874 - 4838

Up from Boredom, Down from Fear

Up from Boredom, Down from Fear

Dr. Bruce Leckart
with L. G. Weinberger

Richard Marek Publishers
New York

Grateful acknowledgment is made for permission to use the following material:

Excerpt from *Waiting for Godot*, by Samuel Beckett, copyright © 1954 by Grove Press, Inc. Reprinted by permission of Grove Press, Inc.

A selection from *Roland Barthes* by Roland Barthes, translated by Richard Howard, translation copyright © 1977 by Farrar, Straus & Giroux, Inc. Reprinted with the permission of Hill and Wang (a Division of Farrar, Straus & Giroux, Inc.).

Cartoon by Jules Feiffer, copyright © 1977 courtesy of the artist.

Anecdote attributed to Sholom Aleichem taken from *A Treasury of Jewish Folk Humor*, edited by Nathan Ausubel, copyright © 1948, 1976 by Crown Publishers, Inc.

"Richard Cory" from *Children of the Night* by E. A. Robinson is used by permission of Charles Scribner's Sons and is fully protected by copyright.

"Foam 'Iceberg' Startles the Aussies" (dateline Sydney). Reprinted by permission of United Press International.

Quote by Max Ehrmann copyright © 1927 by Max Ehrmann. All rights reserved. Copyright renewed 1954 by Bertha K. Ehrmann. Reprinted by permission Robert L. Bell, Melrose, Mass. 02176, USA.

Library of Congress Cataloging in Publication Data

Leckart, Bruce
  Up from boredom, down from fear.
  1. Boredom.   2. Success. I. Weinberger, Lila Gilbreth, joint author.   II.   Title.
BF575.B67L2   158'.1   79–16815
ISBN 0–399–90046–2

Printed in the United States of America

For Skinny

Acknowledgments

I would like to extend my gratitude to a number of persons who contributed to this work, especially my wife, Karen, who provided me with the emotional support, encouragement, and intellectual stimulation needed to complete the project. My thanks to Lilla Weinberger for sharing her remarkable writing talent with me, and to Joyce Engelson, my editor, for believing in me and my ideas and helping make them come true. Thank you, Ed Wohl, for being a good friend and providing me with good advice. May you be blessed with decadence. Thank you, Patricia Denner Cayne, for your assistance at the very beginning of this project. I am indebted to the many students at San Diego State University who assisted in collecting and analyzing the data needed to refine and validate the questionnaires: Tom Carver, Terry Cronan, Karen Hawthorne, Wendy Janda, Cindy Mason, Mike Sandler, and Donna Warlick. Thank you, Rick Stambul and Lew Burger, for taking the time to read and comment on my manuscript. And very special thanks to Adele and George Parker and to Jeanette Chesler.

Contents

Part Two:
Some Conceptual Techniques

3 Dr. Jekyll, Meet Mr. Hyde

1

Boredom: The Big Picture

1 The Fine Art of Making Trouble

This is it. You've taken the first step out of the blues, the blahs, the apathy, the anomie, the everyday despair that so many of us have come to accept as a way of life. You are a potential "troublemaker"—and in my book that's a compliment!

There's an old joke about three men who were arrested and before they knew it, found themselves in front of a firing squad. Asked if they wanted blindfolds the first two donned them eagerly. But the third man refused, whereupon he was told by his comrades: "Take the blindfold, Manny, don't make trouble. . . ."

That's the kind of trouble I mean. Questioning the status quo. Looking at the world your own way. Welcoming a challenge. Creating problems by going out on a limb, then solving them. Trusting your perceptions and dreams enough to follow them, despite lots of free advice to stay home, do the "right thing," watch the tube and, above all, *don't make trouble.*

I've been rocking the boat for a long time now myself (though I had to learn too). And, in some people's judgment, "making a hell of a lot of waves" . . . but also having one hell of a sweet time. We all start out that way, full of zest and curiosity, ready to reach out, take a chance, walk in the rain and get wet, be silly romantics. Then it starts to slip away as we let the guilt and fear imposed on us by others take charge of our lives. Eventually we internalize these feelings and lose ourselves. The rebellions of adolescence are often our last desperate attempts to resist the social pressures to conform. All too soon, as school, job, home and family begin to furnish our years—and just the fact of the years themselves—our lives become thick with convention, our decisions based on "oughts" and "shoulds," our days and nights increasingly dull . . . and finally one day we arrive . . . we are bored! Led around by other people and outside events and institutions, we are told what to feel, what to do, what to think and how to be! Frequently this doesn't work for long and we soon find ourselves going through the motions with a glad face for the world and a heart sinking deeper into boredom or even depression.

As you can guess, my close acquaintance with and understanding of boredom is not something that I have only read about in professional journals and books during my training and tenure as a psychologist. This is something I've lived through too. I began to feel these very same walls closing in on me, threatening to squeeze the life out of my youthful dreams; in fact, it was the fear that I might not be able to escape this fate myself that led me to study what has interested me most for the last twenty years . . . boredom.

At first my curiosity was totally self-centered, restricted to figuring out why I, personally, was feeling this way, and what could be done about it by me, for me. Later, as I got more involved professionally, and became better at coping with my own boredom problems, I extended the scope of my investigation to others, clients in my clinical practice, for example, my friends and colleagues, other species, boredom at school, at home, and eventually to places and people you'd expect to be free of this plague.

The Fine Art of Making Trouble

When it comes to boredom we tend to think that it's a problem that only afflicts those of us in the middle or working classes. One fantasy I've found to be common among many chronically bored people is "If only I could be so and so, rich, famous, and powerful, then, ah yes, *then* I would feel more alive." I had that fantasy myself and spent a considerable number of years chasing it down. But from what I've seen of the rich, famous and powerful in places like Beverly Hills, Monte Carlo, New York, London and so forth, their favorite haunts groan with boredom and are, in their own ways, monuments to the boredom of the people who created them.

Although I'm neither famous nor powerful myself, I've spent a lot of time around those who are, and from what I've seen the fantasy of excitement is just that . . . a fantasy. I've seen great athletes drink themselves into a stupor for lack of a meaningful direction, while in the public image they lead fast-paced lives packed with unending excitement. I've spent time with "successful" lawyers and doctors—people in the vanguard of their professions, the ones you read about in newspapers, magazines and novels—and have heard them discuss their day in court or in the operating room with about as much excitement as you might expect from somebody describing how they had filled in a hole with sand. I've heard people who have made in excess of a million dollars in a single day describe their lives in ways that indicated how truly meaningless their accomplishments were . . . to them.

A real estate broker friend of mine recently completed a four-way twenty-million-dollar deal. His commission will be somewhere in the neighborhood of a million dollars. When he told me about it his voice was flat, his face expressionless. When I wondered why he wasn't happier, he said it wouldn't make any difference to his life. His wife would still complain, it wouldn't allow him to do any of the

21

things he wanted to do, he'd just have the headache of worrying about his new tax bracket. Neither the money nor the deal itself had any meaning for him. And recently I read about Fred Silverman, president of NBC, one of the country's most powerful men, someone whose decisions affect what hundreds of millions of people think about, laugh at, and believe, describe the life of a television executive as "boring—boring! Boring with a capital B."

As I discovered, being rich, famous, powerful, even brilliant does not create an immunity to boredom. Well then, you might be saying to yourself, as I did, "If *they* can't do anything about it, what can I hope to accomplish?" My answer to that is "A GREAT DEAL." First, now you know that being rich, famous, powerful and brilliant doesn't necessarily matter when it comes to boredom. The sense of dull routine and endless drudgery is not confined, it turns out, to the life of a cleaning woman. Second, just how well your life is going—how boring or interesting it is—has to do with the behavior, emotions and attitudes that *you* personally carry around with you . . . and those you *can* look at and do something about.

One reason that most people have trouble dealing with boredom is that no one, professional or amateur, has paid much attention to it, let alone tried to do anything about it. Until now, boredom has received only cursory attention from most behavioral scientists. Compared to other phenomena of human behavior it remains unexplored. The most prevalent attitude has usually been: "Of course I'm bored. Isn't the sky blue? Don't I have to pay taxes?" Well, at the risk of being an optimistic romantic, why don't you start by believing that maybe . . . not for sure, if that is too big a step to take . . . but just maybe, you can do something about pulling yourself up from boredom and down from fear.

Extent of Boredom

Most everyone has experienced boredom at one time or another in their lives and perhaps paid very little attention to it, either not considering it much of a problem, or feeling there was little that could be done about it if it was. But just how important is it? In my experience the larger social consequences of boredom are staggering—accidents, rapes, divorces, murders, suicides, drunk driving, decreased productivity, skyrocketing crime and so on. And on the personal level, the psychological cost is just as great. We see it in the anxiety, apathy, unhappiness and guilt of those around us—people who've lost their zest for living and just give up because "nothing turns me on anymore." Then there are others whose fears have suffocated their sense of adventure until they're afraid to try anything new, those who continue to run for fear of what they may find if they stop, and the misanthropes who hate the world because it has failed to provide them with the perfect mate, the perfect job, with a life that never goes stale.

Erich Fromm suggests that "perhaps the most important source of aggression and destructiveness today is to be found in the 'bored' character." And consider this quote from the Los Angeles *Times* reporting on a gun battle between two youthful gangs. A young man from a ghetto community stops to talk about why it happened: "This happens once a year. . . . You don't have anything. You go to jail, have free grub, eat, get to be with your buddies. Your girlfriend comes to see you. *It breaks the monotony.*"

Then there's one of my patients, Jimmy. At twenty-three he was bright, fresh out of college, and unemployed. There was a smelting plant in his hometown; he'd worked there summers while he was in school. So when they offered him a permanent position he took it. Better than sponging off his parents, he reasoned. He was expected to watch a control panel that monitored the temperature and consistency of the cauldrons of boiling metal down below. But nothing ever went wrong. The plant was so well automated that Jimmy had virtually nothing to do. Eighteen months passed. Then one night after draining a Coke bottle, Jimmy calmly and deliberately sailed it over the edge into one of the bubbling cauldrons. The "entertaining" explosion that followed cost the plant several million dollars.

Look around and you'll see the painful consequences of unrecognized or unacknowledged boredom striking people all around you. Teenagers with more energy than they know what to do with turn to drugs and violence because they haven't figured out what's wrong or what to do about it. Older people with lots of steam left unhappily assume the role of pigeon feeders, watching TV and waiting for senility to overtake them because, not only are they bored, but they have no awareness of the problem, no plan to deal with it, and no belief that things could be better. Poor people with lots of potential find themselves seemingly caught in a boredom-poverty trap. Rich people simply turn to the next immediate thrill currently in vogue, be it the perfect orgasm, an ounce of pure cocaine, a tip on a football game or a handful of barbiturates and alcohol. Then there are the battered wives and children who have committed no particular sin save being in the wrong place at the wrong time; and severely emotionally disturbed schizophrenics mesmerized by heavy doses of major tranquilizers and color TV sinking deeper and deeper into bizarre emotions and thoughts for lack of something meaningful to participate in. People of all types and descriptions kill themselves with overeating, cigarettes, alcohol and other drugs in unsuccessful attempts to feed the insatiable monster of boredom. It's all around, and apparently few of us are immune! It's just a question of how badly we are stricken.

Those who escape some of the more visibly destructive consequences of boredom still suffer from the way it saps their energy, wastes their potential, and destroys their native capacity to have fun, enjoy life, to play a little. My friend Edna, for instance. On the surface she's got it all—everything she'd wanted. But she also got something she hadn't bargained for—boredom. Edna and I went to high school together back in New York. No one expected much of her even then, including Edna herself. But she was friendly and fun—destined, if not for greatness, surely for a small part in the American Dream. At the urging of her parents and girlfriends she dropped out of psychology to become a grade-school teacher. "It's so much more practical, dear." In her senior year of college Ted entered the picture—a future dentist of modest means. Married the week after graduation, Edna helped put Ted through dental school. Their first child was born soon after he set up practice in a thriving suburb not fifteen miles from the neighborhood where they both grew up. Together they set about buying the good life they'd been promised. Cars, clothes, a decorator home. By the time their third child arrived, they were on their second house and going strong. But then something started to give. Life lost its starch for Edna. She tried the standard remedies—bridge, TM, the League of Women Voters—but it was no good. She was bored stiff.

Last time we talked Edna described herself as "uninvolved." "I really don't want anything to happen. I just don't care. . . . When I think about where I am, what I want, and what I'm into I'm not anywhere." As we reminisced, Edna told me how it was when she was younger: "You know, I remember how I felt in 1960—during the presidential election . . . and the difference between then and now is just overwhelming. I couldn't wait to read the newspaper! There was something going on. . . . I can't explain it . . . like pieces of a terribly important puzzle I was putting together. It's not like that anymore. Now it's just plain boring. I haven't even looked at a paper in months."

Edna is in a rut. There's nothing intrinsically boring about the way she lives. When she was thirty she found the same set of circumstances fulfilling. But it's wrong for her at thirty-five. Often boredom signals impending change. It's your body's way of telling you to do something. In Edna's case, she's gone as far as she can go in one direction, and she knows she's bored. But she isn't quite sure what to do about it yet.

One way to get a picture of how much we are all affected by boredom is to try to imagine what the world would be like without it. A bus stop without any bored faces, or a party where everyone actually has a good time; people looking forward to the changes of aging and the challenge of an active retirement; workers who not only want to spend a pleasant evening at home but also want to get up the next morning and go back to their jobs. Friendships that grow and change and sometimes die, but are never dull. A spouse who still surprises you when you least expect it. But most of all, a world of active, curious, involved individuals who aren't afraid to ask questions, explore themselves and their environment and take a few risks.

This utopia I've described would also be free of a lot of social and personal problems we don't usually blame on boredom. In my practice I've found that many of the complaints that bring people to my door, such as alcoholism, incompatibility, depression and so forth can really, underneath it all, be traced right back to boredom.

Joan is a good example. She thought there was something very wrong with her marriage. Not that she didn't love her husband, Steve, but he was just never home. An up-and-coming environmental-protection lawyer, he cared deeply about his work. When he wasn't in the office, he could usually be found in a smoke-filled meeting room enthusiastically plotting the downfall of the city council or the planning commission. Joan found these meetings very dull. So she waited—watching TV, eating alone, wondering what time Steve would be home. Occasionally Joan accepted an invitation for dinner with some old girlfriends. Together they would commiserate—one was married to a football fanatic, another's husband played golf. But none of them thought to question the social conventions that kept them penned up while their men were off enjoying themselves. "All alone by the telephone . . .," they'd been taught to wait since childhood. A woman's place is in the home, after all.

When Joan came to me for help I suggested that boredom might be partly to blame for her unhappiness. In living for someone else she had abdicated her responsibility to provide for her own personal needs. Steve neither wanted nor needed constant attention, and she required far more stimulation than her narrow definition of the housewife's role allowed.

Alcoholism and drug abuse are often just the tip of a mighty iceberg of boredom. One of my patients used to come home, prop himself up in front of the TV and drink until he passed out. And this went on *every night*. He didn't *want* to do it, he certainly didn't enjoy himself, but he'd gotten so deeply entrenched in his boring routine that he'd forgotten how to formulate and carry out other, more interesting activities. Or take Sherry, a young woman who'd tried everything imaginable in the way of drugs and sex by the ripe old age of nineteen. She'd escaped from a dreary small town in the middle of nowhere and a seemingly certain future as a clerk typist in Hollywood, only to find that things looked no brighter for her there. She tried her best to find something meaningful to do, but after a succession of dull, tedious jobs she turned elsewhere for excitement. By the time she came to see me, she'd only just recovered from a near-fatal overdose of heroin.

A sense of depression, too, frequently covers up boredom. Although they are not at all the same, it's easy to mistake one for the other. I recently saw a salesman who was in his early sixties. He'd come to me for counseling because he was having trouble making decisions and felt slightly depressed. His doctor had frightened him into retirement about a year before and he'd dutifully fled to California to lie in the sun. The trouble was he didn't like California, he hated the sun and, although he didn't know why, he couldn't make decisions because he was too bored to care one way or the other. His rather mild heart condition was not nearly as threatening to his well-being as his increasingly acute state of boredom.

Patty saw her problem as one of depression resulting from loneliness. She was convinced that her happiness depended on finding a long-term relationship with a man she could love and respect. She sought him in every singles bar in Los Angeles, but each time she found him she lost him again—usually in a matter of days. Patty had never taken a careful look at why she felt such a desperate need to fill her life with someone else. In large part it had to do with boredom. Her own life felt empty, but rather than looking for a new and more fulfilling life style, she was stuck in a pattern of trying to find Mr. Right—and in all the wrong places.

Boredom Examined

Boredom—and this is very important to remember—can feel like just about anything. Depending on the circumstances, you may feel anxious, angry, depressed, tired, or any number of other unpleasant emotions. It's not until you start to scratch the surface, however, that the real culprit, boredom, shows its face.

Let's look at a common predicament. You're stuck in a very long line, waiting for money, information, assistance—something you need right away. The line seems to be going nowhere. First you look at your watch. Several minutes pass. "This is going to take forever," you mutter to yourself—but loudly enough so others can hear you. Nothing happens. You might then make a thinly veiled hostile comment about the clerk to the fellow next to you. Something like "He must be new because he sure is slow," making certain, of course, that the clerk can hear you. Finally you work yourself up to a really nasty remark directed right at the clerk himself. "Boy, was I mad," you may reflect afterward. But is that what it really was? In fact, you were bored, but boredom that's not nipped in the bud often progresses to anger—or fatigue, or anxiety or whatever. The sad part of the progression is that we have a blow-out with a friend, get anxious over a pseudo-problem (the nearest convenient "problem" that we can drop our discomfort on) or stupefy ourselves with sleep, alcohol and so forth, without ever recognizing that it all started with boredom.

Often, of course, you know you're bored. You're listless, apathetic, uninterested in yourself, others, your surroundings. But for most people the concept of boredom is an end point in their thinking rather than a beginning. For example, I recently went away for a weekend with some friends of ours who brought along their teenage son, Scott. Scott frequently looked unhappy, distant, withdrawn, and when one of us would ask what was wrong, he would reply, "I'm bored." Like most people he had already learned that this was the answer and the end of the conversation. He had said all there was to say and had adequately described what he was feeling, what he was thinking, what he was or wasn't doing and what could be done about it: nothing. Scott soon found out that I was not like most people, though, since I pursued his answer by asking lots of questions (the same ones I've learned to ask myself). First I wanted to know what it felt like. Then what he thought about it, when he first noticed it, what he usually did when he was bored, and on and on. Ultimately we both had an entertaining time as he got involved in the conversation (thus ending his boredom), and I collected a bit more data. I was thoroughly delighted when Scott told me that this was the first time he was aware of having actually done something about his boredom and that he saw he needn't trust its relief to chance. One could *do* something about the grim beast.

What I did with Scott by asking questions and pushing him to look at himself is something I try to do with all people who consult me for one form of boredom or another. When people tell me they are bored and I want to know more about it, I look at three different things and ask three different questions. First, I want to know what they are feeling. Second, what they are doing when they are feeling it. And third, what they are thinking about at that time. By paying attention to these three factors: Emotional-Feeling, Behavioral-Doing, and Cognitive-Thinking, I can define their bored state, which is the first step in helping them come to grips with the problem. We'll take a closer look at these factors in a moment.

Another way to try to understand boredom is to look at people who are bored. What do they have in common? Over the years I've recognized a psychological profile (based both on research data and clinical experience) of the characteristics that are associated with boredom. The bored person is likely to be:

—overly concerned with pleasing others;
—prone to worry;
—lacking in confidence;
—dependent on others;
—anxious for security and material things;
—conforming;
—sensitive to criticism from self and others; and
—afraid of taking chances or making a mistake.

He or she is also likely to have more time available than can be meaningfully used, a highly routinized daily life, and an unexcited mental attitude to both work and play. Somewhat wishy-washy in his or her opinions, the easily bored person usually thinks of work as tedious, and is frequently subject to spells of inertia.

In the next chapter you'll have a chance to take a brief quiz that will help you look at yourself in these areas and give you some idea of the nature and extent of your own boredom.

Boredom Defined

Over an extended period of time I have come to the conclusion that boredom takes many different forms—that you can't describe what it feels like to be bored and then expect it to apply to all people and to all situations in spite of psychological profiles and the like. Each of the different forms of boredom produces a unique pattern of emotions, behaviors and thoughts. Help depends on understanding your own paricular kind of boredom at any particular time and then arriving at an approach that is tail-or-made to address it. There are some general factors, though, which all cases of boredom seem to share.

Emotional-Feeling Indicators

The principal emotional component of boredom is a feeling of uninvolvement, a lack of concentration or focus of one's attention, a loss of enthusiasm, an absence of motivation, a feeling of emptiness and, above all, no excitement or enthusiasm for what is happening. Some people mistakenly describe themselves as being "depressed" but, as we shall see, boredom and depression are quite different. Scott had elements of all these components in his feeling state when we talked. He described himself as not really enjoying what he was doing and not feeling happy, excited or enthusiastic about what was going on. On the other hand, he didn't really know what else to do and didn't feel particularly motivated to move in any other direction. He was caught between not feeling good about what he was doing and feeling at the time, but not really wanting to do anything else that would feel better. This trapped feeling is a characteristic emotional indicator of boredom.

Another way of gaining insight into what it feels like to be bored is to contrast it with its opposite—involvement. When you are involved you are not likely to be aware of your feelings at all. You are too busy. All your attention is taken up, and you with it, by the task at hand, the problem you are solving, the event you are watching, the affair you've just embarked on or the new job you're mastering. Regardless of whether you are a participant or an observer, however, your consciousness is totally focused or concentrated on attending to what is before you. You have no room or time for seeing yourself as a participant, or evaluating yourself or being conscious of how well or poorly you are doing.

A few years ago I became passionately immersed in a game called backgammon, ultimately becoming a world-class player before it started to bore me. It was one of the most engrossing activities I have ever engaged in. The kind of involvement that is the antithesis of boredom was clearly illustrated in an incident that occurred during a game. There was one friend whom I particularly enjoyed playing. Our matches were always tough, close and unpredictable. Early one evening he came over to my house and we started to play. We had been playing for about an hour and it was a good contest with nobody having an advantage. Then, suddenly, I became aware of forty people standing around the dining-room table singing "Happy Birthday." I had gotten so involved that I was totally unaware that forty people had come into the room and surrounded us for *my* surprise birthday party.

Behavioral-Doing Indicators

Behavioral indicators of boredom fall into one of three categories. First is *undirected agitation*. This is most frequently, although not exclusively, seen in children and in adolescents and consists of "nervous" activities that are usually repetitive and not directed toward any particular source or goal. The daughter of a friend of mine typically reveals she is bored by pacing back and forth, picking up one toy for a few moments and making an attempt to play with it, then putting it aside and picking up another only to put it down and make another in a series of false starts. There is no one particular object or activity that commands her attention for any length of time. Undirected

33

agitation seems to be almost random selection of behavior with virtually no purpose or thought behind what is selected. In fact I've come to believe this is how most people deal with boredom, that is, giving very little attention to it as a problem that can be solved by using the same forms of problem solving used to cope with any other psychological difficulty.

Another indicator of boredom is *high rates of repetition of habitual behaviors* like smoking, eating, drinking and a whole host of personal repetitive "fidgeting" mannerisms, such as playing with a mole, rubbing your nose, cleaning your nails and so on. The criterion for distinguishing these behaviors as boredom-induced is that the individual is performing the behaviors absentmindedly, as compared to being attentively involved—and it *is* possible to be involved in cleaning your nails!

The third behavioral indicator is a *lack of goal direction*. We've all seen the fat person who sits down in front of a television set or settles in to listen to some music or read a book surrounded by a vast array of food, only to spend an entire evening eating without really being aware of what he's doing, without even enjoying the taste of the food. It's as if such people are trying to gain some amount of *stimulation* that has nothing to do with taking in nourishment or enjoying the act of eating itself. As we shall see later, this is in fact just what they are doing, and one of the most significant, and as yet undiscovered, ways to weight loss involves solving a boredom problem.

Cognitive-Thinking Indicators

One of the principal cognitive factors present in bored people is their mental confusion and uncertainty about what is occurring and what can be done to correct it.

Ask someone who is bored something like, "Well, John, what would you rather do?" His response is likely to make it clear that he really doesn't know what to do with himself. He has no conscious idea of what will work. People who know what they would prefer to be doing are usually not more than temporarily bored. They may be fantasizing. They may be malingering. They may even be depressed. But they are usually not bored.

One of the primary solutions to boredom problems is overcoming inertia: *just doing something.* Frequently this involves changing the cognitive state of the individual from uncertainty and indecisiveness to a different framework of thought, a framework that replaces uncertainty about what would be pleasurable, and indecisiveness about what to try to do at any given point, with a more adventuresome attitude: "Well, I may not know for certain what to do to relieve myself of this feeling, but I'm going to try something just to get moving in some other direction, since this one is clearly not working for me at all!"

Throughout the remainder of the book the behaviors, emotions and thoughts of people in the throes of one form of boredom or another will be considered. As I've mentioned, a multitude of maladaptive and uncomfortable behaviors, emotions and thoughts are symptomatic of boredom—anger, frustration, drug dependency, obesity, underachievement, self-debasement, discouragement, indecisiveness and confusion are just a few. The techniques for bringing yourself up from the depths of boredom and down from the overstimulation of fear will allow you to cope with these symptoms. For now, however, let me address just one very important question: How is boredom different from depression?

Boredom and/or Depression?

Boredom and depression are not the same thing. Indeed, they are both qualitatively and quantitatively different from one another. There is a major distinction between a depressed person and a bored person: the bored person does not have the *extensive* feelings of guilt, unworthiness, sinfulness, hopelessness, failure and self-blame characteristic of the depressed person. The bored person will experience loss of enthusiasm and involvement, perhaps feel dejected and discouraged, but the extent to which he will blame these occurrences on his own basic worth is limited. The depressive will take that situation and usually come to the conclusion that it is because of his or her own personal limitations, failures and worthlessness that he or she is in this situation. Someone who is bored would not be likely to consider suicide, for instance, whereas a depressed person might. It is only when the bored person starts to flagellate himself, to feel that he deserves whatever he's getting, that this is all happening because he is basically no good, that he crosses over the border from boredom into real depression. Quite likely, many people who ultimately wind up feeling depressed start off by simply feeling bored. Then, due to unknown historical or constitutional factors in their backgrounds, they are unfortunately swept over the border into depression. The techniques that I have devised for dealing with boredom are quite useful in preventing that border-crossing. They help the individual to keep a balance between the roller-coaster-like ride between the low points of boredom and the high points of fear. One of the most fruitful of these techniques involves learning to listen to the crazy things you tell yourself, and then restructuring your internal dialogues or discussions with yourself to reflect your basic sanity. More of that later.

* * *

Earlier I said boredom takes many different forms. As the final part of this initial examination of boredom I'd like to go back and describe these to you, so you can take the first step in doing something about boredom—namely, recognizing and becoming aware of it.

The categories I've formulated here are convenient, if somewhat arbitrary, vantage points for viewing boredom in its various aspects. They are not, however, mutually exclusive, and one category often has something in common with another. For, as we shall see later on, all boredom stems from common sources within ourselves.

Momentary Boredom

Momentary boredom is the simplest and most universal form of boredom. The hallmark of momentary boredom is that it occurs in an interlude between two activities. At some time we all find ourselves sitting in the dentist's office cooling our heels for an hour, trying to work up an interest in a year-old copy of *Field and Stream*, or worse, the *Orthodontist Quarterly*, or waiting for a bus or taxi that just won't come or a luncheon guest who's late. Or standing in line for food, for tickets, for a movie, for any of the thousand and one things we don't have exactly when we want them. The problem presented by momentary boredom is *what can be done to make this time pass more pleasurably*? How can we arrange for these situations to occur less often and for shorter periods of time? And how can we avoid some of the more self-destructive behavior that people, even in these *temporary* situations, often indulge in: fidgeting, extensive smoking, picking at the basket of rolls on the table and so forth. What modifications can we make in our behavior, emotions and attitudes that would make these situations not only less painful but perhaps even enjoyable?

Life-style Boredom

Life-style boredom is obviously more pervasive and severe. Characteristically, some aspect of your style of living no longer gives you the basic gratification, excitement and involvement that it originally produced. In short, you have outgrown your life and failed to notice it. Your job, marriage, location, friends, values, goals or beliefs no longer create a sense of drama, intrigue and involvement. Most frequently, this kind of boredom causes one to feel caught in a rut, apathetic and disinterested in anything his or her world has to offer. The bored person also feels that, although there's no point in doing what he's doing, there are really no other viable, attractive alternatives to it. This kind of boredom feeds on itself and, for some people, becomes a chronic condition. "That's life," they'll say, or, "I guess I'll have to learn to live with it." Eventually they forget that this is *not* necessarily the human condition. They cannot recapture the belief that we are essentially fun-loving, inquisitive, constantly changing beings. And that something *can* be done to put more involvement back in their lives.

Unfortunately for the person with life-style boredom, he is usually not very attuned to himself and is not in touch with what aspects of his life are getting him down. Often people think they know just what is boring them, but because they are out of touch with themselves, they make mistakes. We all have friends who have gotten bored with their marriages and, rather than trying to do something about it, have gotten divorced, only to marry much the same kind of person the second time. From there it's only a

38

short step back to boredom and square one. In the saddest of these cases the unhappiness is attributed to boredom with a spouse and only later it's discovered that the problem was entirely in some other area of life. All the grief and pain associated with the termination of a relationship could have been avoided.

The perpetuation of life-style boredom is almost universally caused by fear and strikes hardest at the individual who has lost touch with his emotions. When this occurs the person is almost invariably aware of the unhappy feelings of life-style boredom without associating them with any particular cause. Many such people are barely aware of their own boredom. They may decide to move on, change jobs or careers, make a radical change in their way of life, only to find that they have been carrying the seeds of their boredom within them all the time. These people have never learned how to find out and deal with what they are really feeling—how to figure out what bores them, and how to work on changing the way they cope with it before they burn their bridges behind them. Of course there are many times when a job, a town, a lover has become boring and this is a genuine signal to change. But not before you've made every effort to understand and alter the patterns that may be pulling you down into an unnecessary boredom of your own devising.

Life-Stages Boredom

Life seems naturally to progress in steps or stages or cycles—in other words, change doesn't occur in a smooth, seamless, continuous way. Rather it happens at predictable times in each person's life (although the outcome at each stage differs from one individual to the next). We move from adolescence to young adulthood. From single to married life . . . and back again. From one career choice to another. From one economic level to another. There seems to be a season and a time for everything.

Life-stages boredom occurs when we get stuck, when we can't seem to make the transition from one stage to the next. When this occurs we are caught in a conflicting situation that doesn't get resolved and, additionally, in a set of circumstances that have lost their exciting properties. Take childbearing, for example. At some point in each couple's relationship there is a time when they decide, either explicitly or otherwise, to have a child or not have a child. Failure to make this decision leads to what Erik Erikson describes as "a pervading sense of stagnation, boredom and interpersonal impoverishment." Once the decision is made the couple is free to pursue a course of action. Indecision, however, leaves them both up in the air. Their future looks uncertain. Not sure what they will be doing they tend to avoid making plans. With no plans there is no movement and no excitement. Life becomes dull, routine and tense until a decision is made, one way or the other.

Most frequently we get trapped in these circumstances by our ambivalence toward change: change is both tempting and frightening. At moments like these it becomes extremely important to have ways of looking at the fears and uncertainties that keep us from moving. We also need an effective set of tools to allow the changes to occur that will bring excitement into our lives and eliminate the drudgery, while keeping our fears reined in.

Relationship Boredom

Boredom in relationships is probably the most extensive and serious boredom problem challenging us. Above all, man is a social animal and his satisfaction with life is mainly determined by how well his relationships are going. Similarly, the positive energy, the spark, that exists or doesn't exist in any relationship is largely a function of how two individuals handle their inevitable boredom with one another—the day-to-day ups and downs produced by mood swings and mundane chores, as well as the long-term effects of spending a lot of time with one person.

Relationships are like people. They seem to have a life of their own; a time for childhood, an adolescence, an adulthood and a period of declining years. This is universally true, apparently, and this knowledge itself is helpful for people who tend to overreact, or to feel guilty, panicky or punitive when a relationship starts to slide or simply to change.

Usually, whether a relationship is romantic or nonromantic, we start out feeling that we have found someone special to be our friend. As the relationship progresses some of the glow invariably wears off and we are left to cope with at least some negative feelings. One of these feelings is boredom. The things that we found terribly exciting at the onset of the relationship seem a bit shopworn and dull. Perhaps they are even a little abrasive. When this happens we are faced with choices and problems. We can either notice what's happening and deal with it, or we can sweep it under the rug. Often people fail to recognize that they are simply bored with one another (perhaps permanently, perhaps temporarily). Rather, when they find something that annoys them about the other person, they make that into a matter of right and wrong and start a battle over who is to change. Other questions that we are faced with are: Should I terminate the relationship or carry on? Is this boredom my signal to end the friendship, marriage or love affair, or can the relationship be changed and the boredom negated and, if so, how? What can I do to recapture some of those high periods? Are both partners bored? How can I cope with the areas that are dull and repetitive—sex, our use of leisure time or the way we seem to have the same conversation over and over again, or no conversation at all? What attitudes do I have that are making it worse for me? Does everyone get bored with other people or is it just me? Different people have different styles of coping with the boredom point in relationships. What is mine and how does it work for and against me? How can I change it in order to feel better?

These and other boredom-related problems that occur in marriages, friendships, sexual relationships, between couples and their other friends, between parents and children, coworkers and so forth will be dealt with extensively throughout the book.

Situational Boredom

Situational boredom is boredom that occurs only when you are placed in a particular situation—a certain task at work you dislike, a tiresome chore at home, the same conversation that you've already had a hundred times with a relative, or a tiresome segment of an otherwise entertaining leisure-time activity—driving through a traffic jam to get to your favorite ski resort, for instance.

A physician friend of mine absolutely loves his professional duties with one exception—filling out insurance forms. No matter how he has tried, there's no way that he can avoid doing it, no way to delegate the responsibility, no way of eliminating the task. The problem is this: What can he do to change his attitudes, make the task less boring or entertain himself while going through the motions, that will be better than his current attitudes, behavior and thoughts about insurance forms? At the moment, the very idea of filling them out produces only boredom and discomfort. Procrastination prolongs the agony. And by the time he gets around to actually doing it, he's not only stuck with a job he hates, but he's got to face a backlog as well.

Many of the things we say we "can't get around to" —whether it's writing letters, cleaning the oven, or mowing the lawn—are tasks that bore us. We avoid them for a very good reason: we don't want to experience boredom. The trouble is, most of these chores can't be put off forever, and the knowledge that they are piling up can sap us of much of the energy we could be using to enjoy the present. Fortunately, there are ways to overcome many of the more unpleasant aspects of situational boredom.

Fear-Induced Boredom

Probably the single most important boredom-producing agent is fear. Many people experience unnecessary boredom because their fears put unnecessary limits on what they will do. At some level they are telling themselves that they cannot accomplish what they want or that doing a particular thing is "not me" while at another level they would very much like to have the experience. Frustrated actors, firemen, skin divers, gamblers or whatever all fit into this category. People who are afraid to reach out and try.

Usually this fear of failing is based on some belief about the likelihood and awfulness of the consequences of failure. We are prone to telling ourselves that our more creative ideas are not only likely to fail, but if and when they do, the repercussions of that failure will be "awful." People susceptible to fear-induced boredom can thus be described as pessimists rather than optimists. Mostly this comes about because in learning to evaluate ourselves the criteria we are taught to apply is too stringent. As a consequence, we tend to anticipate failure and criticism far more than is warranted by the real world, and are thereby needlessly frightened into not taking action. And so we bring boredom down on our own heads.

A friend of mine who is a psychologist and a college professor recently had a difficult time deciding what to do with his future. He had been teaching for about six years; he was respected by his colleagues, admired by his students, and was advancing rapidly up the academic career ladder. One day I was having a talk with him and, to my surprise, he told me that he was having a very tough time working and was feeling depressed about his future. Although he was very good at what he did and had some fun doing it, he really wanted to chuck it all and become a carpenter, an occupation that he had learned from his father and which had supported him nicely through graduate school. We talked a bit about why he didn't do that and it came down to severe self-criticism for "wasting his career," lowering his social position, throwing away something that he had worked for, and disappointing his parents and friends. On top of all that were his fears about being able to make a living at carpentry—an idea that had no basis in reality as he had actually taken a reduction in pay and job security to work as a professor!

Expectational Boredom

When I was a little boy I would frequently put far more food on my plate than I could ever consume.

44

My mother tried to teach me to be less ambitious by pointing out that "once again your eyes are bigger than your stomach." Setting your aspirations too high produces boredom because reality cannot possibly live up to your expectations.

A businessman I was counseling some time ago suffered from this form of expectational boredom. He specializes in taking over small businesses which are having difficulty and turning them around. Each time he takes over a new business he establishes some extremely high expectations of what he can accomplish. At one time he took over a small engine-rebuilding shop and had dreams of turning it into a national franchise. He proceeded first to turn the shop into a local success which, with his experience, was not very difficult. However, when he tried to extend the operation into a national chain he ran into difficulties and ultimately was unable to realize his dreams. He soon became bored with running what was to him a mundane local business and gave it up, although at a large profit. His unrealistic aspirations had once again doomed him to boredom, "failure," and the abandonment of a thriving project. His very real success paled in comparison to his expectations.

Low aspirations can also lead to boredom. People who're afraid of a challenge because they fear their ability to meet it are likely to set their sights so low that there's nothing much to strive for. Their self-confidence doesn't get the boost it needs because they don't ever put themselves on the line.

A woman I know loves to go to school. Every semester she signs up for two or three courses and every semester she claims she's going to try something new. But whenever I ask her what she's taking, it's always Hebrew, Spanish, organ or sewing. She's had all these courses before. She likes the teachers, she says. And she always learns something new. But what about that anthropology course you were interested in, I ask. Oh, I'm not smart enough. I'm much too old to start something new, she says. So rather than welcoming the prospect of facing a teacher and a subject she knows nothing about, she turns back to the known, the safe, the familiar—the ever-increasingly boring.

Closed-Minded Boredom

The world is in constant flux. With each blink of the eye, time changes, your body is different, the environment alters. Sometimes these changes are dramatic, sometimes subtle. But they are constant.

Failure to recognize and respond to these changes results in closed-minded boredom. People hang on to the old because it used to work and shun the new for fear of the unknown. It's more comfortable, more convenient, not to have to come up with a fresh response every time you make a decision—easier to just make the same old decision you've always made. But in the long run, relying on outmoded data is a dead end. It cuts you off from new sources of stimulation and involvement.

Take one of my patients, Angela. She came to see me only because her husband had made it a condition of their marriage that she seek some counseling. She didn't like psychology or psychologists. In fact, Angela didn't like much of anything. Her negativity successfully closed her off from most contact with a world she had early learned to mistrust. Angela had been adopted as a young child after being abandoned by her parents. Her response to this early hurt was to always assume the worst, thereby avoiding any possible disappointments. Unfortunately, this strategy be-

46

came a sort of self-fulfilling prophecy. Because Angela had cut herself off from opportunities to grow and to enjoy herself, she never gathered any evidence that would contradict her closed-minded view of what one might expect from the world. She just sank further and further into dissatisfaction, complaints and closed-minded boredom.

On a smaller scale we all close our minds in ways that cut us off from possible new experiences. How many times have you refused to try a new dish because you *know* you don't like anchovies or eggplant or whatever? Or refused an invitation because square dancing is corny or folk dancing is no fun or ballroom dancing is for old people? Closed-minded boredom flourishes whenever rigid ideas from the past overcome a flexible response to present opportunities for stimulation.

Inertial Boredom

Inertial boredom is boredom maintained simply because there is no apparent or convenient way to break the inertia of doing what you have begun to do, or are used to doing, even though it is not involving or interesting. If you are the type of person who comes home from work, has his dinner, and then goes into the living room and turns on the television without any thought of doing anything else and then bitches and moans about the quality of TV programming and actually does not enjoy the evening ahead, you have a classic case of inertial boredom. The hallmarks of inertial boredom are (1) repetitive behavior, (2) absence of gratification from the boring activity, (3) automatic responsiveness to engaging in the behavior and (4) absence of activity to the contrary despite awareness of

47

dislike. Inertial boredom occurs in sex, in work, in relationships; wherever, in fact, you can imagine being bored.

Stress-Symptom Boredom

Stress-symptom boredom is endemic to the overextended, overworked, overaroused members of our society wherever they are found. As we shall see later, there are people who have higher needs for stimulation than others and who tend to put themselves into situations which generate a lot of stimulation or action. These individuals chronically function under very high levels of stress. And enjoy it up to a point. But when the stress is uninterrupted by periods of relaxation, they are likely to find themselves feeling burned out. If you've been mobilized for action and performance for any length of time, as when you are overworked or overextended, you've probably found that you have very little capacity to become stimulated by anything in your environment. When you are so heavily burdened that nothing seems exciting anymore, you are suffering from stress-symptom boredom.

The question for anyone with stress-symptom boredom is how to reduce the stress enough to recover your capacity for excitement. How do you get away for a while? How can you reduce your level of stimulation long enough to recover? How do you gracefully back off when the pressures are on you to continue? How do you make others around you understand that you need time off? How do you stop yourself from getting overextended next time?

Very often people who are prone to this particular kind of boredom have developed some very successful techniques to ensure that they get the stimulation they need.

Generally they go out on a limb by promising more than they can easily deliver, setting deadlines that are highly optimistic, and creating a high level of expectation on the part of others. Unfortunately, they are not nearly as proficient at figuring out ways to relieve stress once they find themselves no longer stimulated by it.

Intellectual Boredom

One of the common complaints of mothers and fathers who have to spend long periods of time in the company of young children is that they "go crazy talking to people under three feet tall." This is the simplest form of intellectual boredom. In intellectual boredom there is a gap between your intellectual level and the level of the task at hand, the people around you or the demand that your environment places on you. This could occur in relationships, at work, with your best friends and while pursuing some activity that is otherwise engrossing. For instance, I love to teach. It's challenging and involving, and the students are usually unpredictable. But every year at midterm I find myself answering the same old questions about exams. The problem becomes how to cope with the lack of intellectual stimulation by either changing your environment or creating a new attitude that will make the time you must spend in these situations less painful at least and more entertaining at best.

Intellectual boredom often results from the repetition of experience. The first time Uncle Ed told you about how he missed his chance to get into IBM on the ground floor, or your mother recalled your first day in kindergarten, you were probably fascinated. But after twenty years or so, these stories start to pall! The issue then becomes how to change your attitude toward the situation so as to get some new and potentially interesting information from an old source.

Existential Boredom

Existential boredom comes with the belief that in the last analysis there is nothing meaningful to do since, in the long run, what you do hardly matters at all. Even if you were to spend a long time trying to determine the meaning of life and your own part in it, I believe that ultimately you would come to a point where you would have to throw up your hands and say, "I can't find any meaning in all of this" or "If there is any meaning in life, it is clearly beyond my capacity for understanding." Once you've reached this conclusion, you might decide that since there's nothing meaningful to do, then nothing matters, so why do anything at all? Having adopted this line of reasoning, nothing has any importance for you. Everything is boring since it has no significance, meaning or involvement potential. Such an attitude is characteristic of the sufferer from existential boredom.

An alternative to this point of view is to accept that the ultimate meaning of the world is essentially unknowable. Then you can attribute meaning to things that you wish to attribute meaning to without putting yourself on the spot by trying to intellectually defend yourself. That is, you can make choices which, although not necessarily intellectually defensible, are not subject to attack either. In other words, if one is not to feel bored, I believe that, in spite of the unknowability of much of life, one must plunge into it. People need some significance in what they do to satisfy themselves and make it possible to act . . . which is what destroys boredom. But this significance must come from within.

Pseudo-Boredom

There are times in our lives when we all resort to pseudo-boredom. We say that we would rather not do something because it is boring. That is, we use boredom as an excuse. In fact, however, the thing that we are condemning to boredom is not really boring. It's just that, for some reason, we are afraid of it. The student who says that American history is boring may not be experiencing boredom at all but may be afraid to approach his or her studies for fear of failing. The wife who says she is bored with her marriage may be seeking to avoid some painful aspect of it rather than being truly bored. The employee who makes it clear that he finds a particular job boring, which would otherwise be a stepping stone to a better job, may in reality be afraid of failing. How do we distinguish between pseudo-boredom and real boredom? How can you cope with the fears so that you can come up from boredom?

In the early part of this chapter I said that one of the most important ways of coping with boredom involves making trouble, reaching out, taking chances and sometimes getting knocked on your behind. The thoughtful understanding of boredom that we've already begun is only one phase of getting rid of it. Beyond that you have to be prepared to cope with your emotions and, above all, to change at least some of your behavior. (In fact, throughout the remainder of the book I will constantly remind you to pay attention to all three factors: behavior, emotions and thoughts.) But no matter how good your plan, no matter how good and right your ideas, you're going to get set back. The techniques and ideas that follow have worked for me and many others. They'll work for you too, but only if you abandon the safety of your armchair, the cozy confines of the ruts you know, and resolve to strike out for new territory. So you get knocked down. So you don't master it on the first try. So you even look a little silly. So what? You only go round once!

2 Up from Boredom, Down from Fear

VLADIMIR: Charming evening we're having.
ESTRAGON: Unforgettable.
VLADIMIR: And it's not over.
ESTRAGON: Apparently not.
VLADIMIR: It's only the beginning.
ESTRAGON: It's awful.
VLADIMIR: It's worse than being at the theatre.
ESTRAGON: The circus.
VLADIMIR: The music hall.
ESTRAGON: The circus.

—Samuel Beckett, *Waiting for Godot*

In Beckett's famous tragicomedy, two old, yet ageless, tramps languish by the side of the road, unable to act, caught in a net of words. They are waiting: that is their mission in life, their own very personal hell. They are, whether they know it or not, bored; and the play itself is an ode to the inertia of modern times.

But what is there really to know about boredom? One may as well ask what is there to know about breathing?— for boredom is only too familiar to us all. We come across it in a thousand ways each day. Standing in line at the supermarket. Watching the drifting hands of a clock at the office. Hearing the same stale jokes as told by the same stale friends. Even the glorious act of sex can be deadly if you're not careful.

In its most elusive form, boredom can be that vague

haunting sense that all is not right with the world; your shoes don't quite fit and your new Buick with the fancy guarantee stalls more than it should; you'd rather be doing something else, but you're not sure what. Try describing what boredom feels like to you. Not so easy, is it? Very often we don't even know *when* we're bored or *whether* we're bored, let alone what to do about it.

Boredom Survey

Not long ago I devised a handy way to give you an idea of how bored you really are. It's very simple: for each of the statements just enter the number that corresponds to the answer that's most correct about your life at this time. For example, if you feel that statement number 1 is *especially true* about you enter the number *5.* If you feel that it is *true* about you enter the number *4.* If you feel that it is *neither clearly true nor false* enter the number *3.* If you feel that it is *false* enter the number *2,* and if you feel that it is *especially false* enter the number *1.*

5 = especially true
4 = true
3 = neither clearly true nor false
2 = false
1 = especially false

1. My daily schedule is too predictable. _____

2. My hobbies have lost some of their initial excitement although I still continue to engage in them. _____

3. My job's responsibilities and duties seem tedious and repetitious. _____

4. I don't seem to be learning much at work these days.   _____

5. I am not very stimulated by the people I am friendly with.   _____

6. I have a lot of free time on my hands that I cannot seem to fill in exciting ways.

   _____

7. Sunday is an especially bad day for me.

   _____

8. I often feel that I am wasting a lot of my time.   _____

9. I don't often strike off on my own to find something new, but wait until introduced to it by someone I know.   _____

10. Being successful at my job is very important to me.   _____

11. I do not have any particular passions or strong beliefs.   _____

12. I am especially sensitive to making mistakes.   _____

13. Being lost is a frightening experience that I would do almost anything to avoid.

    _____

14. I would not be very likely to go to a "consciousness raising" group.

    _____

15. Most of the people I socialize with are very stable and dependable.   _____

16. It doesn't seem to make much difference to me if my work gets done or not.

    _____

17. I would not invite someone to lunch whom I did not know well.   _____

18. If I didn't know if I could do something I probably wouldn't try. _____

19. I would be very uncomfortable if my friends thought I was a little "weird." _____

20. My sex makes it difficult for me to do things that I would otherwise find fun. _____

21. I have deeply regretted having taken chances which didn't work out to my advantage. _____

22. I am often afraid to try things because I may appear childish or foolish. _____

23. I tend to go along with the group rather than to make my own desires known. _____

24. I would be unlikely to leave an old, unsatisfactory job unless I had a similarly secure one to go to. _____

25. I don't often look for new and innovative ways to do routine required tasks. _____

26. I am given to periods of depression. _____

27. If I'm alone I find it difficult to amuse myself. _____

28. I do not have enough confidence in my abilities. _____

29. Winning seems much more important than playing. _____

30. I am more a creature of habit than a creature of free will. _____

31. I do a lot of things that don't really interest me. _____

32. I spend a lot of my time worrying.
_____

33. It often seems less important to please myself than to please others. _____

34. There are often lots of things I have to do but don't really feel like doing. _____

35. I have a lot of free time that I can't seem to utilize meaningfully. _____

36. I often feel like there is something that I would like to be doing but I just can't seem to put my finger on what it is.
_____

Scoring

1. Add up the number of questions that you answered with a *4* or a *5*, that is, with a *"true"* or *"especially true."*
2. If your score totals more than 10 or 11 you are probably someone who is frequently bored. The number 10 is somewhat arbitrary, of course, so even if you find your score is less than 10 but still close to it, chances are that boredom is a significant issue in your life.

Interpretation

The purpose of this questionnaire is not to give you an absolute measure of the precise amount of boredom you're experiencing, nor to show how you stack up against the "average" person. Rather, it's to give you a rough estimate that will allow you to compare your experiences with the experience of lots of other people. All the questionnaires in this book have been tested on a large nationwide sample, and these questions have been found to be statistically significant in discriminating between people who experience a great deal of boredom in their lives and those who do not. Still, no test is absolutely foolproof.

A second and major purpose of the test is to give you some food for thought. You can use these questions as a starting point for some thinking about the particular aspects of your own thoughts, feelings and behavior that relate to boredom. With a bit of reflection you'll be able to increase your awareness of whether or not you are really bored—your life may turn out to be more interesting than you thought! If you do have a boredom problem, how severe is it, how does it manifest itself, how does it limit you?

We know that we've all been bored at some time or other in our lives; sometimes we know that we are experiencing boredom in the present, but what is it exactly, where does it come from, and what are some of its manifestations? These will be the major concerns of this chapter. We'll be looking at boredom from the standpoint of arousal theory—a way of viewing one's feelings, thoughts and actions. We'll also take a quick look at some of boredom's symptoms and consequences—for many of the things we do that lead to unhappiness can be better understood as misguided attempts to elude either boredom or fear.

Elementary, My Dear Sigmund

For years the closest thing we had to a psychology of boredom was the motivation theory conceived by Sigmund Freud in the late nineteenth century. Freud, after studying medicine in Paris and Vienna, had intended to go into pure research (his first love was neurology). Circumstances conspired, however, to lead him into private practice instead. Sidetracked but not derailed, Freud worked with the "neurological" material at hand, analyzing himself and the complaints and dreams of his patients. Eventually he arrived at a new explanation for human behavior, and a new treatment—psychoanalysis—for personality disorders. Underlying all the legendary Freudian concepts (id, ego, superego, etc.) is his theory of motivation, which holds that behavior is the result of a need to reduce nervous tension. "The nervous system," Freud wrote, "is an apparatus that seeks to reduce excitation to the lowest possible level, an apparatus which would even, if this were feasible, maintain itself in an altogether unstimulated condition."

How would this work in practice? Well, suppose the body needs food. According to Freud, this biological need is translated into excitement in the nervous system—a sensation we've learned to identify as hunger—which, in turn, stimulates us to make a midnight trip to the refrigerator or perhaps the local deli. Once we've had our fill of hot pastrami or cold pizza or whatever, the need is reduced, and the nervous system returns to its familiar lethargy.

Times changed, however, and with them changed the approach to truth. Most of Freud's theories were soon challenged by a new school of thought, behaviorism. Led by men like John Watson, Clark Hull and B. F. Skinner, the behaviorists weren't much interested in dreams or feelings or subjective personal experience. They wanted to prove that psychology could be an exact science—a structure based on factual observation and carefully supervised laboratory experiments. People and all their problems were best avoided. Rats were far less troublesome, the behaviorists argued, and so much easier to control.

Oddly enough, however, where motivation was concerned these two schools found themselves in perfect accord! Messrs. Watson, Hull and Skinner would, no doubt, have looked askance at the nineteenth-century Viennese hausfrau as a data base, while Freud might have been equally dubious about the contribution of a white rat to the understanding of human behavior, but the two schools agreed that motivation was merely a matter of keeping the nervous system in a state of minimal arousal.

When diagrammed, the theoretical positions of the Freudians and the behaviorists look something like this:

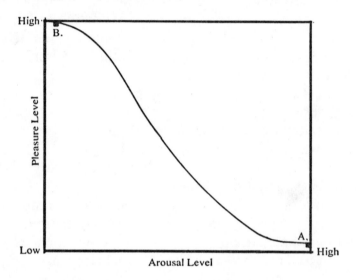

Figure 1: Arousal and Pleasure according to the Arousal Reduction Theory

When the level of arousal or excitation is high, pleasure is low (point A) and when the arousal level is low, pleasure is high (point B). Decreasing the level of arousal when it is high *increases* pleasure, whereas increasing the level of arousal *decreases* pleasure. This is now known as the *arousal-reduction theory* of motivation or, as it is sometimes called, the drive-reduction theory. For its time it was a clear, even elegant, explanation of both animal and human behavior.

Over the last thirty years, however, evidence began to accumulate that could not be so elegantly explained. The rationales became tedious and complicated, and in science, when a theory has to be modified beyond recognition to conform to the observed facts, that theory's days are numbered.

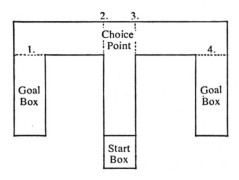

Figure 2: Top View of an E Maze

In one of the classic experiments in animal learning a hungry rat is placed at the bottom of an E maze. (See Figure 2.) It wanders up to the crossbar where it has two choices. If the rat goes to the right it gets a reward—a few pellets of food—but if it turns left it is quickly removed and placed back on square one. This procedure is repeated over and over again until the rat learns through trial and error that a right turn always results in a treat. At this point it stops exploring to the left and turns right 100 percent of the time. A perfect illustration of arousal-reduction theory, right? Depriving the rat of food creates a tissue need which in turn leads to excitation in the nervous system. This stimulates behavior that reduces the need and consequently the excitation.

Back in the early sixties, however, an experiment I conducted with Dr. M. Ray Denny in the animal psychology laboratories at Michigan State University made for quite a different story. Using an E maze we blocked access to the left-hand side of the maze with a closed door and proceeded to condition the rats to turn right for their dinner. Once they knew where the food was, the door to the left was opened. Despite the fact that they were quite hungry, 100 percent of the rats chose to explore the unknown rather than eat!—a choice which had absolutely nothing to do with the tissue need we created by withholding food.

But rats weren't the only heretics. In his tests with schoolchildren, the noted psychologist Donald Hebb demonstrated how vulnerable the arousal-reduction theory really was.

"All of the 600 odd pupils in a city school," wrote Hebb, "ranging from 6 to 15 years of age, were suddenly informed that they need do no work whatever unless they wanted to, that the punishment for being noisy and interrupting others' work was to be sent to the playground to play, and that the reward for being good was to be allowed to do more work. In these circumstances, *all* of the pupils discovered within a day or two that within limits, they *preferred work* to not working."

Both the laboratory experiments with rats and Hebb's studies of children point to the same conclusion: living things (be they rats, humans or walruses) do not live by bread alone. Without a little spice the mind wanders; we look for a way out. We adopt what psychologists have called "exploratory behavior"—a term for the natural curiosity in us all.

It's remotely possible, I suppose, that even in the face of this sort of learned opposition, the arousal-reduction theory might have limped along for years without falling into disrepute were it not for the Korean War. Psychology and psychological warfare reached new heights of sophistication in Korea. In part this was due to the public's ambivalence about the conflict. The cause of the war was just too abstract for many Americans: we were being asked to fight the Chinese—the same Chinese who barely five years before had been perceived as "heroes" and "good guys" in all the cinema newsreels. As would be echoed later in Vietnam we were not there to "win" so much as to "contain." There could be no winners in such a conflict, only losers. And the biggest losers of all, it turned out, were the American prisoners of war.

As we watched the parade of POWs recanting their "sins" before Chinese and Russian television cameras it became clear that the whole subject of motivation would have to be reassessed. Why were American prisoners breaking down? What kinds of torture were the Chinese using to make them turn on their country? Among government officials and in the press there was a lot of loose talk about "brainwashing" (the forcible application of prolonged and intensive indoctrination) and another related technique: sensory deprivation.

Sensory-deprivation studies really began to blossom in the shadow of Korea and the cold war. Government grants were generously dispersed to find out not only what was going on inside Chinese prison camps, but also to combat the monotony that was part and parcel of the new age of war. We'd come a long way from throwing spears at one another. Now there were rockets and hydrogen bombs to contend with, and a radar operator might spend long hours alone in a dark room watching interminable blips on a screen. The consequences of failing to detect a signal on the scope, or reporting a blip that wasn't there, could spell Armageddon. We had to learn more.

One of the earliest sensory-deprivation experiments was conducted by Drs. Bexton, Heron and Scott at McGill University in Montreal. They paid students twenty dollars a day (a decent wage back in the 1950s) simply to lie on a comfortable bed and do nothing. That's right—nothing. They were asked to wear translucent goggles which allowed them to perceive light but not patterns. They were also given cotton gloves and cardboard cuffs to reduce any touch sensations. The testing room was relatively sound-proof and there were short periods throughout the day when they could eat and go to the toilet.

The results of this experiment were astonishing. After just a few hours of isolation, and sometimes in as little as twenty minutes, the students began to go to pieces. They became irritable, confused, frightened; their thoughts were jumbled and incoherent. As time went on many started to hallucinate: the testing room was filled with light, they said; there were dots, they said, and lines and geometric shapes and ultimately full-grown landscapes such as they had never seen before. Not one would endure more than a few days of this sort of agony—at any price.

What, exactly, were the students being deprived of? What could possibly create such discomfort when all their physical needs had supposedly been met? The answer is that we all require *stimulus change*. Without it we go mad—and quite quickly too.

The requirement for stimulus change seems to be built into our nervous system at the simplest level. The work of Dr. Walter Cohen provides just one of the many demonstrations of how essential stimulus change is to even our simplest normal functioning. Using a Gansfeld—a sphere one meter in diameter painted white on the inside—he bathed the interior in a saturated red light and had his subjects peer inside. Although the red light continued unabated, in about three minutes' time all sensation of color had disappeared. When asked what color they saw, the subjects reported the light to be gray. Apparently, if the stimulus is not changing even the simple process of perceiving color cannot go on.

The lesson then is clear: *We need change to function.* Without some input our intellectual, perceptual and emotional processes deteriorate rapidly. The mind is just like any other tool in that respect—leave it out in the rain and it will rust.

Arousal Theory

Stimulus change produces arousal. It feels good, it's exciting, it creates involvement. Ultimately, solving a boredom problem involves understanding, cultivating and exploring sources of change.

Anything that takes you by surprise excites the central nervous system. It alters the patterns in your brain waves and produces dramatic—and desirable—changes throughout the body.

Not too many mornings ago I was in my car, driving downtown, just minding my own business, when suddenly out of the corner of my eye I noticed something peculiar. The fellow in the Toyota one lane over wasn't quite the right shape. He seemed too large for the driver's seat. And his hair—his hair was a shock of yellow. Not blond, mind you, but *yellow*—dazzling, frizzy, electric yellow! Then he glanced in my direction and, my God, his face was covered with white paint. Big red tears dribbled down his cheeks. My first response was intense interest mixed with mild panic. A lunatic, I thought. A lunatic who's staring at me. God knows what he'll do next. But a split second later it all fell into place. *Warren the Clown*, the orange letters on the car door spelled out. Just another commuter on his way to work.

When the arousal level changes a definite sequence of physiological events are set in motion. In this case my behavior was characteristic of a pattern known as the *orienting response*. Any new stimulus causes us to turn, or *orient*, toward the source of arousal. We want to know what it is.

At the same time, our body prepares us for "fight or flight" in case we're in danger. Our pupils dilate, letting in more light to increase the chance of detecting a potential threat. Muscles tense up. Brain waves become more rapid, the heart rate changes and breathing is deeper and less frequent.

If arousal is too high, as it was when I couldn't put the clown into any sane frame of reference, it's experienced as fear. Once I'd identified him correctly, however, and no longer felt endangered, I could enjoy the novelty of the experience. I'd moved from an uncomfortably high state of arousal to a more moderate level where I was pleasantly intrigued.

If we were still stuck with the old arousal-reduction theory (where lack of arousal was thought to be accompanied by an increase in pleasure) I'd presumably be even happier once the clown had passed and everything returned to normal. But no. Warren the Clown had made me realize just how dull a freeway could be. I played with the radio. Nothing doing. Read the billboards until I couldn't tell a Kent from a Tareyton. By then I was almost downtown and my thoughts turned to dodging traffic and the meeting I was heading for.

The arousal theory of motivation says simply that we need to be *moderately* aroused. When there's nothing going on we get bored. When there's too much happening, we panic. And that's ultimately the solution to any boredom problem—finding and maintaining an optimal level of arousal by getting the right amount of stimulus change for you. When you've been getting too little stimulation you need to learn how to get more so you can feel better by coming up from boredom. If you've been getting too much stimulation you need to learn how to come down from fear, overarousal and anxiety.

The relationship between arousal and pleasure is shown

in Figure 3. The right-hand side of Figure 3, you'll notice, looks just like Figure 1. Here, pleasure is inversely related to arousal. The left side of the diagram, however, represents a departure from the old notions of arousal reduction. And it's this side of the figure that deals with boredom.

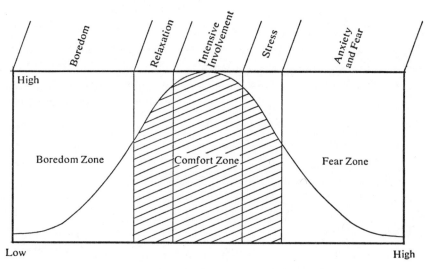

Figure 3: Arousal Level and Pleasure According to the New Arousal Theory

When you're in the boredom zone you're not getting enough arousal and life loses its pizzazz. You feel unexcited, uninvolved, un–just about anything. Your mind wanders. Like as not you'll be tired and restless at the same time. This aimless casting about for something to do is the motivating force that, if heeded, will lead you to seek some form of stimulus change that will take you out of the doldrums to a more comfortable level of arousal.

At the other end of the spectrum we find fear. Far from boredom, but also far from pleasant. Fear is either learned or innate. Excessively loud noises produce an innate fear response called the *defensive reflex*. It's characterized by flinching and cringing—similar to the orienting response, but much more intense. Very few fears, however, are innate. Babies, when they are physically hurt, take far longer to react to pain than do adults. That's because they haven't learned to expect it—it takes them by surprise. By the time we reach adulthood, however, most of our fears are learned responses to situations that are not, in themselves, innately fear-producing. We're conditioned to anticipate that any injury will result in hurt, for instance; and, in fact, we usually overreact, remembering past accidents rather than paying attention to how we're feeling in the present.

Often, by putting an otherwise neutral topic in close proximity to something that already produces fear, the two become inexorably tangled together. In one of the classic experiments in psychology, dogs were taught to associate food with loud noises and painful electric shocks and, therefore, to avoid it. A child for whom the dinner table is the scene of frequent family fights may develop a similar unpleasant association with food. Sometimes the things we're afraid of have been lost in the netherworld of the subconscious; we experience the emotion without remembering its cause. This is known as free-floating anxiety. Your heart palpitates, you start to sweat, your blood pressure shoots up and you're overwhelmed by a feeling that something awful is about to happen.

In the middle of the arousal continuum is the happy medium we're all striving for—not too scared and not too bored. The comfort zone, let's call it. You could be doing just about anything here—from reading a good detective story to having sex to shooting the rapids. But whatever you're doing you're in the present tense—not reliving the past or daydreaming about the future. And it's *you* that's in the present doing what makes *you* happy. Not what your Aunt Esther or Uncle Harry told you would or should make you happy.

One of the nice things about this state of mind is that it's not only pleasant, it's efficient. An overwhelming amount of psychological research has proved that with a modest amount of excitement performance hits its peak. Stage fright is one example. Most actresses and actors depend on it to give their performance an edge. Athletes, too, require a certain amount of stress to do their best. Too much anxiety, of course, will have just the opposite effect. In sports there's a common but barely studied phenomenon called "the choke." An athlete seems to be on the verge of winning when he's overwhelmed by the notion of getting something he badly wants (and maybe never really expected). What does he do? He chokes up. He forgets how to swing his racket. His legs lose their bounce. It's over. On the other hand, an athlete who has absolutely no interest in the outcome of a game will also do poorly.

Why We Get Bored

Habituation

Habituation is by far the most significant boredom producer. To understand this process let's look at an experience we probably all have in common—the flowering of a new friendship. You find each other in the photocopy room at work or at a family party—someplace you'd never expect to meet a kindred spirit. But you both know right away that this is special. Here's someone who's got a new slant on things, who makes you think, who shares your interests, who not only gets your jokes but actually finds them as funny as you do. You're both excited, stimulated, high on the electricity you're generating together. Of course you arrange to meet again. And again, and again. Now, depending on the two of you, the second, third or fourth meeting may or may not be quite as exciting as the first. But it's just about guaranteed that somewhere in the course of your friendship you'll begin to catch your first glimpses of boredom. Maybe it's because you've fallen into the habit of dinner once a week—always the same restaurant, always on Thursday night. . . . Or maybe you've heard the same funny stories once too often. Your friend has become a known quantity. You no longer wonder what he or she will do next, or where this new relationship will lead you. All the exciting things they do begin to pale the second and third time around. Stimuli, regardless of how exciting they are initially, lose the ability to create arousal with repeated exposures. *Your arousal level is minimal because habituation has reduced the arousal-producing effects of the situation to almost nil.*

Let's look more closely at what this means in practice. In some situations familiarity can be a plus. Try to remember your first day on the job—any job. There's so much to learn, so many new faces to remember. You can't help but wonder if maybe this time you won't be up to the challenge. Your head swims, and the day goes by so quickly that it's over just as you begin to realize where you are. It would be neither possible nor desirable to maintain this arousal level for long—you'd soon be a nervous wreck. Now think back to how you felt, after, say, a month at that same job. The procedures were starting to make sense. And you knew everybody's name by heart . . . and their dogs' and their kids' and their pet rocks'. . . . Habituation can take the sting out of new and frightening situations. But it also reduces the exciting to the mundane. It can bring us down from fear but, if we're not careful to monitor it and take remedial action when necessary, it can also bring us down from the comfort zone and into boredom.

A few years ago my wife and I exchanged houses with friends from the East for a couple of weeks. I'd gotten tired of blue skies and palm trees, and they were eager to escape from snow country for a while. When we compared notes on our respective vacations they'd had a wonderful time, except for the refrigerator noise. It nearly drove them crazy, they said. "What refrigerator noise?" we asked. "That high-pitched whining sound . . . probably a bad compressor." Suddenly I could hear it loud and clear. How could we have lived with it all this time, I wondered, and never noticed?

Anyone who has ever lived near a railroad track or airport knows that we adjust quite quickly to the most atrocious interruptions of our peace and quiet. Now this is an advantage where trains, planes and whiny refrigerators are concerned, but in dealing with boredom it's a drag. For we not only habituate to the small annoyances of life, we also get used to its pleasures. Childhood friendships, husbands and wives, favorite books and records, even cherished daydreams often lose their bloom with time. "I'm too old for that sort of thing anymore," we say about ourselves or (to others), "Act your age." Almost as if we wanted our husbands and wives and daydreams and the whole joyous cosmology to fade! It can, of course. And so subtly that, before you know it, you're up to your ears in boredom.

71

Preconceived Notions

Another reason we get bored has to do with the rigidly held beliefs, the closed-minded prejudices and preconceived notions about all sorts of things, that we bring to our experiences.

At one time or another we've all dreamed of finding ourselves alone on a desert island. Sunshine and coconuts, a grass shack by a blue lagoon . . . lots of peace and quiet. You can almost hear that ukelele plink-plink-plinking in the background. The perfect way to spend a weekend. But what about Monday, and Tuesday, and the day after that? Soon your little retreat would seem more like Alcatraz than Bora Bora.

The charm of such a fantasy lies in our stereotype of the desert island as such a simple place that there is virtually no opportunity for stimulus change. It's a place to relieve stress-symptom boredom. We turn to it for solace when civilization gets to be too much for us—when our arousal level is sky-high. But what if you were really stranded there?

The degree of complexity in our environment is, of course, one of the determinants of boredom. The more there is to do in any given situation, the more chances there are to shift gears and thereby change your arousal level. In an impoverished environment like our clichéd desert isle, your options would be severely limited.

Fortunately, boredom is not just a function of our environment. If it were we'd have very little control over it, since we all find ourselves in situations now and then which appear to offer nothing in the way of stimulation. Life is chock full of these dead spaces. Or is it?

Complexity works because it provides us with more opportunities for stimulus change, but complexity, I've learned, depends largely on your point of view, on the images and expectations you carry around with you. You can create your own opportunities for stimulus change. If you were a marine biologist, for example, a desert island might be an ideal spot for observing sea anemones or estimating the shark population in the surrounding waters. All an astronomer need do is crane his neck and he's right at home. Even a psychologist would not be entirely without resources. Like Freud, if push came to shove he could always lie down on the beach and analyze himself! But just about any of us can find something of interest the minute we stop thinking of our circumstances as inherently boring. It's the preconception, more than anything else, that numbs us.

How many, for instance, would be intrigued by the notion of playing Parcheesi? "A children's game," I hear you say, "not sophisticated enough for adults." And yet, in a slightly altered form, this game has turned perfectly sensible, intelligent people into raving fanatics, zombies obsessed with only one thought—another game of backgammon. The rules of this game are, indeed, child's play (they can be learned in a matter of minutes) but, for aficionados, it is a matter of enormous subtlety. Some of the greatest gamesmen of our time have spent hours engrossed in passionate debate on the merits and drawbacks of a single move. One computer programmer I know used to spend all his spare time trying to work out the answer to a fairly simple backgammon problem. Sixty thousand dollars' worth of computer time later he still wasn't sure! But he'd gotten his money's worth in excitement, involvement and a good measure of stimulus change.

Predictability

I have a friend who blows the punch line to every joke she tells. The other day she began to tell a story

73

I'd heard a million times. Ordinarily there's nothing worse. The same old buildup to the same old predictable conclusion. But with Lucy it was different. I was in suspense from the moment she began, wondering how she'd manage to botch it up this time. And, as usual, her version was even funnier than the original.

When there are no uncertainties, no possibility of surprise, when everything is secure, boredom reigns supreme. And yet we're all half convinced that that's what we should want—security at any price. Well, let me tell you, for one thing you can't buy it. Change occurs no matter how hard we try to exclude it from our lives. And even if you could have it, you wouldn't want it for very long. To come up from boredom we need to learn to seek out, cultivate and cope with change rather than fear it. Instead, most of us have used predictability to reduce our fears and, in the process, have overshot the comfort zone.

The more regular and predictable the environment, the less interesting (arousal-producing) it is. Consider, for a moment, the casinos of Las Vegas. What are they made of? Glass and glitter. A few free drinks and a lot of loose change. Why are they so popular then? Because it's hard to predict what may happen to you when you step inside. You could get lucky, after all. It happens all the time in Vegas. Take what has to be by any stretch of the imagination a boring, idiotic activity—yanking the arm of a slot machine over and over. Not all that different from the tedium of any other assembly line, is it? Now introduce an element of chance (for instance, a few lemons and cherries and oranges to reflect on in various combinations). Mix in a small financial incentive and presto! you've created a pastime as American as Howard Hughes.

Entertainment, in fact, is largely suspense. We read to find out what happens. Who done it and why. Surprises. Incongruity. The bizarre and the unexpected. In terms of stimulus change, suspense works here by leading you to expect one thing and then surprising you with another. Television writers tear their hair week after week trying to come up with a fresh slant. A kung-fu master who wanders around the American West. *Star Trek. Perry Mason. Name That Tune. You Asked for It.* The whole trick is to keep us guessing. Remember how quickly *The $64,000 Question* fell from grace once it was revealed that the show was rigged?

In sports, the issue of who will win and how they'll do it keeps fans on the edge of their seats. Here suspense occurs because we have high hopes but relatively few expectations. In other words, the outcome is uncertain. When uncertainty is removed altogether the game goes flat. Sports promoters are well aware of this fact and do everything in their power to preserve the aura of unpredictability. In the 1976 Forest Hills U.S. Women's Open Tennis Tournament, for example, Chris Evert and Yvonne Goolagong were so superior to their opponents that they weren't allowed to compete in the main stadium until the finals. The preliminary matches, said officials, would be just too dull.

Unpredictability in sex is, according to many couples, the element they miss the most. Before they settled down, they say, there was always the question of whether to go to bed with someone, and where and when and what it would be like. In the good old days anticipation was half the fun. Once the sequence of seduction becomes inflexible, both partners begin to sense something lacking.

Extramarital affairs are often a direct result of this boredom in bed. The unknown elements of an encounter—what will he or she look like in the nude? How does she make love? what's he going to do next?—provide much of the excitement. And then, of course, there's always the secrecy, and the consequences of being found out. For many people the possibility of discovery is no small part of the thrill.

75

Brad chose to incorporate as many surprises as possible into his marriage instead of looking for it outside. He was a forty-five-year-old bachelor when he met his wife, Faye. For twenty-five years he'd been playing the field, never spending more than a few weeks with the same person. Inevitably he'd get bored and move on to greener pastures. He's been married now for two years—a record as far as he's concerned—and although the relationship is far from conventional, it seems to be working for them. The secret lies in utter unpredictability. The other night, for instance, they were sitting in the living room watching TV when Faye burst into tears, convinced that Brad no longer loved her. A few weeks earlier she'd gotten bored and went to see her sister for a few days, not telling him where she was going or why. Brad finds this unsettling; after all, he's used to having the upper hand with women. But so far his discomfort has been offset by his curiosity. He never knows what's going to happen next. Their household, though stormy, is never boring. Whether the excitement will continue to compensate for the pain remains to be seen, but for now they're still together where calmer, more traditional relationships have long since gone by the boards.

Playing It Safe

Recently I met an electronics technician who had a very well-paying job with plenty of security and fringe benifits, who was about to give it all up to form his own solar heating company. He was refinancing his house and borrowing large amounts of cash from his family and friends in order to support a venture that was anything but sure-fire. Listening to him I got to thinking about the importance of laying your life on the line every once in a while. There's no surer road to boredom than continually playing it safe. It doesn't matter much what's at stake, as long as it's personally important to you.

Take the stock market, for instance. Banks, bonds or even under the mattress are probably better places to put your money . . . and yet people each year breathlessly invest their hard-earned dollars on Wall Street. Naive? Perhaps. Bored? Almost certainly. The lure of the market is not its quick payoff, but rather the sheer risk involved. Sure, you stand to gain. But the chance of losing is just as great, if not greater.

All kinds of human activities depend on this risk factor for their interest. In the waters off Japan there is a deadly poisonous blowfish called *fugu*. The Japanese are immensely fond of this fish and long ago they devised a means of extracting the poison from the gland of the *fugu* before eating it. But, being an aesthetic people, they take great care not to remove all of the poison. There should be just enough left, they say, to make your lips tingle. That's part of the thrill. Cooking, however, is an art, not a science, and even good cooks have bad days. Should you be so unfortunate, therefore, as to eat some poorly prepared *fugu* fish, you will die within hours, for there is no known antidote. The Japanese are not unaware of this eventuality. Yet every year millions indulge in the exotic taste of *fugu* and, for a small percentage of these, *fugu* is their "last supper."

From a psychological standpoint there seem to be two distinct sources of satisfaction in this kind of serious gambling. First, there's the kick of beating the odds, completing what you set out to do without losing your shirt. And second, there's the knowledge that you've succeeded in avoiding boredom without becoming overaroused—or scared to death! Each of us has his or her own individual tolerance levels, of course. What's risky for one person may be duck soup for the next. The feat is to live in such a way that you're always testing your own limits, pushing out against the temptation to arrange a life for yourself that's so comfortable there's no challenge left.

Overdoing It

No matter how habituated a subject may be to flashing lights, loud noises, rubber hammers or any of the other harrowing experiences psychologists impose, give him a little rest, try it again, and sure enough, you'll manage to make him jump once more. And the longer you wait the higher he'll jump. In scientific terms this means that the more time that elapses between exposures to the same stimulus, the stronger the response becomes. It's the same way with boredom. Whatever you're doing, stop. Take a little rest. Then try it again. You'll be amazed.

I like to spend some of my spare time wielding a paint brush—not on a canvas, mind you, but on walls and ceilings. Changing the color of a room does wonders for my morale. I know from experience, though, that I'm only good for about two days of hard work. After that I get restless, ready to move on to other things. So usually I try to pace myself to finish in two days or less. Never more. As I clean my rollers and stretch my aching back I always wonder whatever made me think this was any fun. But even then I know that as the weeks pass I'll forget and the urge to transform my environment will hit me once more.

Many activities follow this cyclical pattern, although the frequency rates vary considerably from person to person. Take tennis, for instance. I can play tennis for days in a row, then find one morning that the urge is gone. It may not return for months. As with the stock market, all things, even friendships, have their highs and lows, and managing boredom depends on becoming aware of these very natural cycles in our attention spans and giving them their due.

Whether you've got to do your income tax or mend your socks, try remembering that there's no inherent virtue in wallowing in boredom. You can do a little bit at a time, pacing yourself in order to take advantage of whatever interest you have in the project.

Noting your own particular rates of recovery from habituation is very helpful in coping with boredom. Start trying to pay attention now to when you need stimulus change in different areas of your life. Later on, in Chapter 4, you'll have a chance to measure the amount of stimulus change you require to stay in the comfort zone of arousal.

Boredom Unmasked

Like syphilis, boredom is a quiet malady, a master of disguise. People may suffer for years and years without even knowing they are bored, just treating symptoms or, worse, palming their misery off on someone else. Distress and pain, of course, are only signals—the body's way of announcing that something is wrong. And with a little help from the American drug industry you can muffle these signals almost immediately. But not without consequences. Perhaps it's true that five milligrams of Valium will take the edge off an anxiety attack, but can it really cure a lackluster marriage or get you through another day at the office? I think not. The causes of boredom tend to be long-term, and those who jokingly complain of "terminal boredom" are often far closer to the truth than they might otherwise care to admit.

Owning up to being really bored is sometimes more difficult than declaring oneself an alcoholic or a drug addict or a compulsive eater, in part because people feel that somehow they should know, innately, how to deal with it, in part because boredom just isn't taken seriously. Bored people, after all, are thought to be no threat to society. They simply stay that way. Alcoholics, on the other hand, get behind the wheel of a car and become murderers. And drug addicts, as everyone knows, will do almost anything to support their habits. Compulsive eaters? Well, they kill themselves. All these people have places they can go for counseling and rehabilitation. They have, over a period of time, legitimized their plights, and therefore are well on their way to dealing with them. Boredom sufferers remain trapped in the Dark Ages, however. Their problem is generally neither specific nor acute enough to warrant a visit to a psychologist's or psychiatrist's office (although, once all the frills are removed, boredom turns out to be a major problem for a large percentage of my patients). There are no halfway houses for the bored. Nor are close friends and relatives much help, since they often have a vested interest in maintaining the status quo. The bored person is left to try to cope alone. There is little to guide him in his search for answers since so few people have even recognized that a real and important need exists. Very often, either because it doesn't seem socially acceptable to complain of something so "trivial," or because they don't really know themselves why they feel so bad, people mislabel their boredom—most often as frustration, depression, fatigue or some form of self-destructive behavior—and thus mistake the symptoms for the problem itself.

As we have seen, boredom which goes too long unappreciated or misunderstood can result in serious personal and social costs. Self-destructive and socially destructive behavior results when people lose touch with what they're really thinking and feeling and doing. It's as though (to borrow from a television cliché) an "invisible shield" has risen around you. You're in a kind of exile, isolated from your true self. You say you've got a headache or you're worn out, but that's not what you mean. And since you don't know what's really troubling you, how on earth can you take responsibility for it? The answer is simple: you can't. Someone else has to do it for you. Your husband, perhaps, or your wife and children. Or maybe your boss is the culprit. Or society itself. It's easy (and inevitable) to try to place the blame on someone or something else. That's how marriages break up. How kids drop out of school. How people drift aimlessly from one job to another, failing, always failing.

Understanding boredom's many faces can help you place the responsibility back where it belongs—on your very real and legitimate physical, mental and emotional needs for stimulus change. But what happens when these needs aren't met? We get frustrated. Why, then, don't we just go out and get ourselves some stimulation? We'll examine the answer to this puzzling question next.

2
Some Conceptual Techniques

3 *Dr. Jekyll, Meet Mr. Hyde*

"As a child, I was often and intensely bored. This evidently began very early, it has continued my whole life, in gusts (increasingly rare, it is true, thanks to work and to friends), and it has always been noticeable to others. A panic boredom, to the point of distress: like the kind I feel in panel discussions, lectures, parties among strangers, group amusements: wherever boredom can be seen. Might boredom be my form of hysteria?"

—Roland Barthes

The connection between boredom and frustration that we've already started to explore is one of the keys to understanding why we do, feel and think some of the crazy things that keep us swinging back and forth between boredom and fear. In this chapter we're going to take a closer look at how we're conditioned to act in ways that frustrate our need for stimulation, the way this conditioning splits us in two and what our crazy half does that keeps us locked into boredom.

Boredom is the child of frustration—of being stuck in the same rut for more years than we care to remember. But where does frustration come from? Well, some of it (a minuscule amount), is built into our environment. There are just too many variables, too many things in this hectic, overheated world of ours that can go haywire. Technology offers only the illusion of utopia; it cannot shield us from reality. We ought to know that by now.

You've packed the kids off to Grandma, cashed your vacation check, made reservations at the Hilton and left plenty of cat food behind for Agamemnon. You're on your way to the airport and you're holding hands again for the first time in thirty years—all set to fly away to Bermuda on that second honeymoon. Your hearts are pounding wildly as they used to do in high school, when over the radio comes the word: Hurricane Hilda: 200-mile-per-hour winds. Bermuda no longer exists.

Random events can throw a monkey wrench into anyone's plans. The frustration that results from being trapped in an elevator for nine hours with twelve stockbrokers is inevitable. But it needn't produce boredom as well. There's nothing to be done, no one to blame. The best you can hope for under these conditions is to adopt the "long view."

In 1977 an Air India jet en route from New Delhi to Bangkok was taken over by political terrorists and forced to land in Bangladesh. The plane sat on the ground for two days in the sweltering heat while the terrorists waved hand grenades and issued ultimatums and government officials played for time. Among the passengers on board were a group of Sufis (Islamic mystics). When the hostages were finally released it was observed that of all those involved, the Sufis were the least affected by the ordeal. They had taken the long view. If Allah willed that they die in Dacca at the hands of strangers, they told reporters, and for a cause they knew nothing about, well then, that was perfectly acceptable to them.

Some of our frustration is the handiwork of others. There are always a few people, it seems, who, for one reason or another, stand in the way of what we want. Your next-door neighbor (the one with the Great Dane) who insists on using his chain saw every Sunday morning. The clerk who's stealing you blind as part of his private war on capitalism. The landlord who is always there on the first of the month, but never when you need him.

There's nothing random about this sort of frustration. It is direct and personal, and what's more, there *are* things you can do about it. You can buy a book on assertion training and learn some clever retorts. You can move away from neighbors with Great Danes and chain saws. You can fire a clerk who's stealing from you, even have him arrested if you like. And for every fair-weather landlord there are three attorneys more than willing to drag him into court.

But the bulk of our frustration has nothing to do with the mechanics of the external world. It comes, rather, from within ourselves. In spite of our native intelligence and curiosity, we've been conditioned to think, feel and act in ways that frustrate us—ways that keep us from maintaining an optimal level of arousal. Why is it so hard for people to meet what ought to be a perfectly natural biological need? Animals in the wild are never bored—at least not for long. But then we're not animals. We're human beings— conscious human beings—and that makes all the difference.

We can look at what we're doing while we're doing it. We're capable of logical thought. We can collect information and draw conclusions from it. And having drawn a conclusion, we can act on it. So far so good.

But there are limits on our ability to know. We can't always gather all the information we need in order to arrive at sound, rational decisions, for one thing. We collect most of our information from our senses—and the senses are only capable of a narrow range of perception. The eye, for instance, cannot see infrared or ultraviolet light rays. The ear can pick up sounds only within the middle of the tone scale. And even within this narrow range, there are limits to the amounts of information we can process. We see and hear far more than we consciously comprehend. We're also restricted by the numbers and sophistication of the concepts available to us. No matter how intelligent, a person living in the Middle Ages could not appreciate the potential danger of a live wire because he wouldn't know the first thing about electricity. Nor could that same person understand the use of antibiotics without a crash course in modern medicine. Finally, we're all biased and bound by the values our culture builds into us from a very early age. We eat with a knife and fork and spoon, not with our fingers. We walk on the sidewalk. We don't read other people's mail, and generally we'd rather wait to have our babies until after we're married. Just because we're conditioned to accept the values of our own time and place doesn't mean we always abide by them, however. Most of us are only "semisocial." We have stronger values than we are capable of executing. That is, there's a discrepancy between our social expectations and our ability to live up to them.

One of the areas where we are most restricted is in understanding the causes of our own behavior. When asked, most people can come up with a plausible reason for why they go to work everyday, or why they are majoring in history as opposed to political science. But often this is just a smokescreen. It has little or nothing to do with their real motivation. Not that they are lying. They simply don't know themselves. With a little time under their belts and a bit of gentle prodding by a trained psychologist, the truth will bubble up to the surface. People who say they married for love but really just wanted to ditch their mothers. People who've spent their whole lives building financial empires out of a desperate need for approval. All those things you would have done differently if you'd only known then what you know now.

And there are things we do for reasons which never surface. Or for reasons which have long been forgotten. Feelings, thoughts and actions that bypass the conscious, rational self completely. Why are some people terrified of mice, say? They don't bite. They don't eat much. And they're soft and furry. The ideal house pet. But generations of children have grown up with parents who shriek at the sight of one. There must be something threatening here, the little tots conclude, and by the time they're adults they've forgotten why they're afraid. Still, the fear lingers on. These learned responses are instilled in all of us as we grow up. And they affect not only our response to mice, spiders and the like, but also our attitudes toward ourselves and the world. From patriotism and religion to how to blow your nose, you've been conditioned to accept certain ways of doing things as *right*. A great many of the things that we take for granted are a result of our cultural conditioning. And to the extent that we neglect to question and examine these assumptions about ourselves and the world, the more likely we are to take a very limited—and boring—view of our options. Because as soon as you stop and think about it, it's obvious that new facts are being discovered every day, and there are a million different ways to approach just about every situation—no one of which is absolutely best.

Much of the way we respond to any given incident depends on our point of view at that particular time in our lives. And points of view can always change. . . . The Buddhists, for instance, say that there are four responses to every issue, and they've been studying mankind and his attendant pain as long as anybody. Let us illustrate. The issue is drinking: You are fresh out of Sunday school and have never had a drop of booze in your life. But you know people who have . . . friends who go out regularly on the town and get smashed and seem to have a splendid time doing it, so naturally you're curious. And before too long your curiosity gets the best of you. One night suddenly there you are, shuffling up to the bar with all your pals, smiling from ear to ear, downing martinis like an old pro. You get high. Very high. Too high, in fact. And the next morning you wake up feeling as if you've been hit by a milk truck. I'll never do that again, you promise yourself. For months afterward you shun alcohol altogether. When someone says let's go for a beer after work you shake your head. "I've changed my mind about drinking," you say with a moral streak in your voice. Depending on how traumatized you felt by that first experience you may never touch liquor again. Usually, though, your resolve will weaken with time, and a new debate will begin inside your head. I don't have to be a saint, you reason. But there's nothing wrong with social drinking, is there? No . . . as long as it stays that way—social, not serious. Everything in moderation, that's all. So you shift into third gear. Now you're a careful drinker. One of those people who are forever clamping their hands over the wine glass just as the waiter starts to pour another round. Like the teetotaler, this moderate viewpoint may also endure. But usually there comes a time in your life—prompted perhaps by a wedding or a divorce or a death in the family—when you'll truly want to get drunk. Even though you know good and well what the consequences will be. It is then, according to the Buddhists, that you'll have come full circle, having touched on all four responses. But just think of the many points of view you've taken along the way.

Of course, many of our cultural assumptions are there for a good reason. They help us get through the day without constantly agonizing over whether we're "doing the right thing." But these very same values can also get us into trouble. Take loyalty to "God and country," for instance. Most of us like it here. We're comfortable where we are. We don't dream every night of running off to the Soviet Union and we wouldn't hesitate to proclaim our allegiance to our homeland. At the same time we'd all much prefer to stay alive. So if a draft notice arrived in the mail we'd be faced with a difficult decision. The fact that so many in this dilemma traditionally choose to serve is just one measure of how strong these built-in beliefs can be. On a more mundane level, consider your social obligations. How many times have you found yourself surrounded by boorish, obnoxious people—people you'd rather not see—just because you "owed" them an invitation, or because it was easier to say yes than no—and so much more polite!

Taking stock of the areas where your particular conditioning is strongest is a good place to start combating boredom. But how can you do this for yourself? Aren't these blind spots just about impossible to pinpoint? A fish, it is said, has no awareness of the water it swims in. So far we've been assuming that we're dealing with only one person—you. The same you who feels great one morning and awful the next. Who's creative, energetic and unbeatable one week and bored, tired, down in the dumps the rest of the month. Can this person really be one and the same?

The Crazy Me and the Sane Me

In 1957 a tremendously popular book called *The Three Faces of Eve* was published. It was all about a woman who had three separate and very vivid personalities. More recently in the same vein there was *Sybil*, an in-

91

triguing story of another woman who was plagued by no less than sixteen personas—all within the same body! These women were not possessed by the devil, nor were they schizophrenic—at least not in the strict, clinical sense.* This form of illness is diagnosed as a kind of hysteria, but the fascination that these women's stories hold for so many has to do with the recognition that none of us have completely integrated personalities. We are all composed of different selves.

Maybe these selves aren't as distinct as Eve's, nor as numerous as Sybil's, nor as cut off from one another as either, but they're surely familiar. Let us consider some of the irrational fears, urges and beliefs that people we've known have at times allowed to run their lives. One friend of mine, a promising young real estate broker, had to change careers in midstream because he developed freeway phobia. A woman I know refuses to take a vacation because she's sure something is going to happen to her aging parents while she's gone. And we've all met people who've set a goal for themselves, almost reached it and then blown it at the last moment for fear of actually succeeding. Recently I talked with someone who'd just failed the bar. She'd gone to law school after her family had left the nest, done extremely well, and then, the night before the bar, developed insomnia. Desperate, after a sleepless night, she'd asked a friend for something to help her through the exam. She took a Dexedrine but it only made things worse. By the time she started thinking clearly again, it was too late. She'd already sabotaged what was, the day before, an almost certain triumph.

---

*Schizophrenia refers specifically to a split between the emotional or affective process and the intellectual process. Diagnostically, cases of multiple personality are classified as hysteria.

Dr. Jekyll, Meet Mr. Hyde

But I'm not like that, you say. I'd never do anything so irrational, so self-defeating. Perhaps not. But then again, what is it that keeps you from maintaining a level of arousal in the comfort zone at all times? It doesn't take much. A careless word or action now and then is all that's needed to plunge you into yet another bout with boredom. We've all had cause to wonder, time and time again, why am I doing this? Whatever came over me? You've gotten yourself stuck in yet another boring situation and, in retrospect, it seems clear that whatever you did was definitely not in your best interest. "I wasn't myself" is the common excuse. But isn't this a contradiction? How can "I" not be "myself"? If you weren't yourself, who were you? A split personality—what I call the Crazy Me and the Sane Me—is part and parcel of us all; it is the price of admission to the twentieth century.

The Crazy Me is not the same for all of us, of course. Mine leans toward paranoia: strangers looking to do me in for no reason at all, colleagues coveting my favorite courses, thieves and muggers watching my every move. . . . Yours may be partial to isolationism—"If I go out in the world I'll get hurt"—helplessness—"I can't do anything right"—and so on. But in spite of their different aspects, our Crazy Me's have a lot in common. To start with, they're wrong. They have a view of the world which has very little to do with reality, and a lot to do with their own fantasies. These fantasies are responsible for a great deal of the unnecessary misery and discomfort we all experience. When you get bent out of shape for no reason at all, when it takes you days to make a relatively unimportant decision, when you find yourself worrying about things you can't do anything about, that's the Crazy Me coming out of the woodwork. Feelings of inadequacy, guilt, uncontrollable anger, depression or suspicion—all can be laid at the feet of the Crazy Me. Ultimately, the Crazy Me is the manifestation of some mistaken but deeply held beliefs about the world. These beliefs not only stand in your way as far as feeling good and liking yourself are concerned, they also keep you from getting involved, from reaching out for what you want, from creating a new and livelier existence. In other words, *they are directly responsible for your boredom.*

Going Overboard

The Crazy Me is not only unrealistic, it's also extremely rigid. There are no in betweens, no gray areas. Frequently the assumptions of the Crazy Me could be exactly reversed and you'd still be no saner. Take the issue of responsibility. As far as the Crazy Me is concerned you're either totally responsible for everything or else you have no responsibilities at all.

Refusing to take responsibility can get us into a lot of frustrating binds. Once upon a time we all had someone else to take care of us. All we had to do was wail and we were fed and changed and cuddled and coddled. As we grew up we learned to ask for what we wanted, but there was still someone else there to provide it. Now if you're tired there's no one around to tell you to take a nap; if you're hungry you've got to make your own peanut butter sandwich. But it's still tempting to wait and hope that your problems will be solved by someone else. Old habits die hard. Almost anyone can play the role of Mama—your boss, your spouse, friends, relatives, even total strangers! But sometimes nobody wants to play, and then you get into absurd little dialogues such as this:

94

Dr. Jekyll, Meet Mr. Hyde

"What would you like to do tonight?"
"Oh, I don't know. Whatever you'd like to do."
"Well, I don't care. You decide."
"No, you."

And on and on and on. Neither party wants to make a decision because it might not work out. Then they'd be to blame for a boring evening. Failing to accept responsibility for yourself is usually a form of fear-induced boredom. But what are we afraid of? We're afraid that if we really try to get what we want we'll botch it. Better to sit around doing nothing than to, God forbid, make a mistake. At least this way no one can point the finger. Underlying this attitude is the notion that any behavior that falls short of perfection is sure to lead to disaster—a throwback, no doubt, to our infancy when we didn't yet understand the rules. We knew that some actions brought praise while others got us a quick swipe on the behind. But which was which, that was another question. So out of this early anxiety we "learned" that mistakes could, quite literally, be painful. Such timid thinking leads to fantasies of rescue by Prince Charming or Wonder Woman—someone who will do it for us, who will provide the spice and glitter that's lacking in our lives. But fantasies like these can never be actualized. Back here on earth things plod along, just as they always have. The house payment due next Thursday. The laundry that won't go away by itself. The car that needs another tuneup. There is no cavalry galloping over the hill to put an end to all this. Your boredom is your problem, and no one else's.

Taking too much responsibility for events over which we really have no control can also lead to boredom. A few years ago I saw a woman who was suffering from inertial boredom. She was deeply upset by her son's refusal to serve in Vietnam. He had fled to Canada, leaving their entire community in an uproar. It was a quiet, conservative little town where that sort of thing just wasn't done. His mother, Claire, instead of recognizing that her twenty-year-old son had started to make his own decisions, took the responsibility for his action on herself. She indulged in such a storm of self-recrimination that the rest of her life came to a standstill. She dropped her classes at the local college, let the garden go to hell, and went into a first-rate slump. By stopping all her outside activities, Claire just about guaranteed her own boredom. A feeling of inertia soon followed, and Claire's incessant self-criticism kept her from the knowledge that she had a right to fulfill her own needs for stimulation.

Claire spent six months in therapy exploring why she felt like the universe and all its contents had fallen on her shoulders. Finally she was able to see that although she disagreed with her son's stand, she was not to blame for it. She was, however, to blame for her own unhappiness, and for that of her worried husband.

Claire was a victim of the "where did I go wrong" fallacy—the illusion that no matter what happens, it's all your fault. Often, whatever goes wrong has nothing to do with anyone. It's just the way the cookie crumbles. But many of us have gotten into the habit of thinking that there must be someone to blame, and the most logical candidate seems to be you-know-who. Besides, it's a good way of wriggling off the hook. If everything is your fault, then you'd damn well better not do anything until you figure out where you went wrong, so you can avoid it the next time. The only trouble is there may not be a next time. Many chronic cases of inertial boredom originate right here. Wallowing in your own guilt is often so absorbing that it precludes any meaningful involvement in anything else.

Toeing the Line

The Crazy Me imprisons us with lots of "oughts," "shoulds," "do's" and "don'ts." Paying too much attention to all these rules and restrictions will lead you right into the rut of life-style boredom. When we were smaller and still somewhat savage our elders did their best to teach us the ways of civilization. The trouble is that most of them did such a good job of it that we're more in touch with what others think than with our own desires. We end up living someone else's idea of who we are—an idea that has nothing to do with our actual talents, interests and urges. And often this "someone else" exists only in our minds—a ghost from childhood that should have been exorcised a long time ago.

I have a friend, Jean, who's been working for the government for six years now. She's very good at her job, respected by her colleagues, and well on her way up the civil-service ladder. I'd never thought to question whether she liked her work. Then, the other day over coffee, Jean told me she was thinking about quitting. In spite of her experience, her status as one of the up and coming young experts in her field and a salary that was way beyond what she could hope to earn on her own, she'd been dreaming of going to India to set up her own export-import business. As it turns out, Jean was sensing the initial onslaught of life-style boredom. She'd traveled a lot just after college and found that her taste for adventure far exceeded the two- or three-week vacations she could take from her job. Besides, while she liked the money and status she had, she was bored with the actual work. It had all become routine long ago. "I'd rather be back in India," she said, sighing, "with the beggars and elephants and that sense of never knowing what's going to happen next." At least part of her wanted to be there. . . .

But the other part of her, her Crazy Me, was putting words in her mouth, telling her that she really "ought" to stick it out. "On the other hand," Jean said, "I'm not really suffering, and my family and my boss would be so disappointed. Besides, I'd be wasting my potential, throwing away something I'd worked hard for. . . ."

This aspect of the Crazy Me I call the Prosecuting Attorney. Essentially, the Prosecuting Attorney wants to make us feel guilty. "There's something inherently wrong," he tells Jean, "with wanting to go to India. You know it and I know it. Now stop acting like a nineteen-year-old hippie."

As we talked on, another aspect of the Crazy Me took the stage. Call him the Prophet of Doom. His part is to scare Jean with all the "what ifs." "Of course, it might be tough to start my own business," Jean worried, "and the money wouldn't be steady. . . . I wouldn't have any health insurance or retirement benefits to fall back on . . . and what if I changed my mind?. . . I couldn't face going back."

Guilt (the Prosecuting Attorney) and fear (the Prophet of Doom) live within us all. They keep us from following up on the leads we're continually getting from the Sane Me. In fact, it's not exaggerating to say that most of the time we're in a state of war: our bright, rational self who recognizes the symptoms of life-style boredom and is willing to risk a change versus our conformist self who doesn't want to do anything to upset the apple cart. And when the Crazy Me is the victor, boredom also wins the day.

Sometimes the effect of all the restrictions that are placed on us as children is just the opposite of what was intended. Rather than conforming to our parents' wishes we rebel. This is a trap of a different color, but the net effect is the same.

One of my patients, Michael, came to me with a drug problem that was really more a life-style boredom problem. The son of a well-to-do physician, he'd broken away in his early teens from a family that had achieved material success at the expense of personal happiness. Vowing to avoid that fate no matter what, Michael set off on a fifteen-year trip, bouncing from commune to commune and drug to drug. He stayed high most of the time; this kept the straight world at bay, but it also meant that he was never himself long enough to explore anything that might challenge his superior but undernourished intellect. Finally, when he reached thirty, he came to terms with the fact that he was bored. The sixties were played out, he had a good forty years to go, and all he knew how to do was deal dope and panhandle.

Together we explored the limitations he'd imposed on himself by adopting an allegiance to rebellion that was just as uncompromising as his father's insistence on making it. Once he was able to see much of his nonconformity as a reaction rather than an expression of his individuality, Michael could begin to explore those aspects of the world that really turned him on—regardless of their labels.

Conformists and nonconformists alike respond in old and inappropriate ways to a world that in fact is always new and fresh. Reevaluating these knee-jerk reactions is an important step toward gaining control of your life and thus overcoming boredom.

99

Being Careful

All of us are driven. Sometimes by hope, but more often than not by fear. Fear of rejection. Fear of pain and death. It's encoded in the "wisdom" we blithely pass on to our children: "Don't talk to strangers." (Translation: "Strangers are always dangerous.") "Don't change horses in midstream." (Translation: "Never change your mind, even if you know you're wrong.") Or, perhaps most devastating of all, the vapid advice to "be careful." As though the moment you step out the door you're going to find yourself on a tightrope overlooking an abyss. The timid, suspicious, tentative stance that these generalized fears engender make it very hard to take the kind of positive approach to new experience that combats boredom best.

Fear, of course, has been and will continue to be an invaluable mechanism in the survival of the human race. It's built-in, just like hunger. When something threatens we automatically become fearful. The adrenalin starts pumping. The heart beats overtime like a canary's. That's good. That's healthy. As long as there is really something specific out there to be afraid of—a mad dog in your front yard, a lynch mob, a sniper, a tornado. . . .

But the trouble with fear is that it's always there—just below the surface—whether you need it or not. And unless you've woken up to just who you are and what you want out of life, fear will drive you in the most conservative—and boring—direction possible.

Herb and Veronica have been married for twenty-nine years. Twenty-nine miserable years of relationship boredom. They knew it early on, but they thought that things would smooth themselves out in time. Then the children came along and their differences went underground "for appearances' sake." But that was a long time ago. Their

100

children have grown up, they've gone off on their own and now it's open season once more. "Herb drinks too much," she says. "He's never taken me anywhere except to bars." "Veronica is a nag," he says. They stopped sleeping in the same bed three years ago. Their lives are consumed by a grim domestic ritual. Every evening after dinner Veronica disappears into her room to sew, while Herb falls asleep in front of the television set. She doesn't much like to sew. And he never really pays attention to the television. But it's better, he thinks, than whatever's playing at home. At least it puts him to sleep. Herb and Veronica are not fools. They know good and well that they're bored and unhappy. They've talked about getting a divorce. But somehow, they just can't. They're afraid. "What will our children think of us?" Veronica wonders. (Translation: "We will be disgraced. I'm afraid I couldn't bear that.") "Who will take care of me?" asks Herb. "I don't want to be alone." (Translation: "I'm afraid that I'm incompetent.") Veronica and Herb have a chronic case of relationship boredom. And they know it. The odd thing is that, in spite of their mutual pain, the boredom they know seems preferable to the alternative—facing a new and unpredictable future. Were it not for their mutual fear of change, Herb and Veronica could either part or start looking for a different and as yet unexplored basis for their marriage.

Irrational fear keeps us strapped in all kinds of ways. How many times have you heard the following: "Gee, going skiing could be fun, *but* I might break my leg." Or: "I'd sure like to visit Mexico, *but* what would happen to me if I got sick? A strange country . . . I don't speak the language. . . ." Or: "I think I'd enjoy taking acting classes *but* I'm afraid I'd just make a fool of myself." There may be some validity to all these fears. You might break your leg going skiing. And you might very well find yourself in a difficult situation if you took ill in Mexico. It happens, sure. Not often, but once in a while.

One simple test of whether you're acting irrationally is to ask yourself: *Is my fear proportional to the risk?* Sometimes there may be no way to satisfactorily answer this. But most of the time we can call on our intelligence to provide us with a reasonably accurate guess. Acting on what we know, however, is something else again.

Airplanes, for instance. They've been around in one form or another now for three-quarters of a century. They've been studied and flown and written about in more ways than anyone thought imaginable. They are perhaps as emblematic as anything of the twentieth century, a "known" quantity if there ever was one. You take off, sit for a couple of hours and you land. The technology is all in place. Over long distances flying has proved to be a safe, cheap, efficient means of travel. The chances that you'll be killed in a commercial plane crash are about one in a million. If you were to take the same trip by car you'd be ten times more likely to die. Yet every year, millions of people balk at the thought of traveling by commercial airliner. They stay at home. They mow the lawn and watch travelogues on television rather than spending their week's vacation in Hawaii. They know all the facts about airplanes, but their Crazy Me's are not about to be swayed by the facts. Thus fear-induced boredom wins yet another round.

Closed-Mindedness

If there is a critical difference between one who is "opinionated" and one who is "closed-minded," it's that while both believe in the rectitude of their points of view, the opinionated person recognizes that his is ultimately just a "point of view." A closed mind, on the other hand, will grant you nothing. Closed minds are never buffeted about by facts or opinions. They imagine that they can anticipate how they will react in any and all situations. It isn't simply that they presume to know themselves— they presume to know *everything.* And the reason they know everything is because, for them at least, time has stopped. It's very neat but not very interesting. What they see is what they want to see—no more, no less. As a direct consequence of their closed-mindedness, such people are invariably bored.

A man with closed-minded boredom knows, for instance, that he wouldn't enjoy going to a baseball game. How does he know? "Well now," he might retort, "you just tell me what's so damned exciting about watching some idiot with tobacco in his mouth try to hit a round ball with a round stick and then run around a square?" It may have been twenty years since this person last went to a baseball game. Perhaps all he can remember about it now is that the last time out it wasn't much fun. The hot dog he ate was stone cold, or someone spilled a beer on his lap. Whatever happened that summer's day back in 1959, it just wasn't worth repeating. Now, certainly, he could be right. But it's equally possible that he's dead wrong.

The inevitable result of closed-mindedness is boredom. You know exactly how you feel about this, that and the other thing—therefore there is nothing further to discuss. Baseball and your reaction to it is predictable. Politics? Democrats, Republicans, Socialists, Communists . . . they're all the same underneath. Seen one politician and you've seen them all.

Fortunately, this kind of rigidity is learned. And whatever we've learned, we can also, with a good deal of effort, "unlearn."

Not long ago I was having lunch with some friends in a coffee shop. One of the women brought her four-year-old daughter with her. The table was crowded with hamburgers, fries, Cokes, coffee, milk and other amenities. No one was feeling particularly imaginative that day except for the four-year-old. About halfway through the meal she turned to her mother and asked, "Mommy, can I put some milk in my Coke?" Milk and coke, I thought. Together? What a horrible idea! Luckily, her mother was more open to the possibility. "Well, maybe," she said. "Let's try a little bit and see how you like it." She asked the waitress for an extra glass. One part Coke, one part milk. Stir gently with a spoon and serve. The little girl took a sip of her concoction and beamed. "Good!" she said, pushing the glass in my direction. "Taste it!" Rather than go into a diplomatic song-and-dance ("No thanks, I like my milk neat" or words to that effect) I took a cautious sip. She was right. It was light. Bubbly. Different. I found myself suddenly coming out the other side of the argument, insisting that everyone else at the table try it and see.

This experience was a useful reminder to me of how easy it is to fall into closed-minded boredom. None of us are sufficiently flexible to consider ourselves immune to the dangers of rigid thinking.

Pie in the Sky

A few years ago I was invited to attend a Japanese tea ceremony. I'd always wondered what all the fuss was about. Making tea had never seemed a very elevating task to me. Just one of the many mundane chores that interrupt the important things of life, I thought.

When I arrived at Mrs. Okada's I was asked to remove

my outdoor shoes and put on a pair of slippers. I stepped from the entryway into another world. The flowers, the utensils, even the view from the window were carefully chosen and beautifully arranged. As the ceremony progressed I became aware of the quiet economy of each movement. Mrs. Okada seemed relaxed, yet totally involved in what she was doing. The mere act of making a cup of tea became a dance, a meditation on the beauty in the commonplace. Everything about it was timeless—that is, perfectly balanced in the present. It needed no justification to sustain the grace of bowing, pouring and serving. It simply *was*.

I left ready to throw away my recycled teabags and cracked cups and begin to live for the moment. But it's not so easy to discard the habits of a lifetime. I know. I still find myself daydreaming now and then about what I'm going to do when I'm elected President of the United States. At some level we continue to believe in all those fairy tales we digested at our parents' knees. "When I grow up I'm going to be a great doctor . . . a brilliant lawyer . . . a perfect mother. . . ." Now, in and of themselves, these little fantasies can be quite entertaining. Who can fault a five-year-old who wants to be an astronaut? But when we begin to think that we *have* to become astronauts before we can be happy, there's trouble brewing, and this trouble takes the form of expectational boredom—boredom induced by impossibly high aspirations. If wealth and fame are prerequisites to fulfillment, then any role that doesn't explicitly lead us in those directions becomes, ipso facto, boring. Washing dishes, parking cars, answering telephones all day long—nobody wants to make a career out of these kinds of jobs. Why? Because they are boring. And why are they boring? Because they have nothing to do with the romantic pictures we have painted of ourselves. For in our mind's eye, each of us is a hero, a dark star shuffling along through the supermarket checkout line. Sensing this schism in us all, the pop artist Andy Warhol once jokingly predicted that in the world of the future, everyone would be famous for fifteen minutes.

But worse than having goals that are too high is having no goals at all, or goals that are too easy to attain. This is the other side of expectational boredom—people who are afraid to expect anything for fear that they'll be disappointed, or people who've set their sights too low. Quick success can freeze us in our tracks, and it's more common than most people think. Quite often as we reach middle age we find, much to our surprise, that we've "made it." We've achieved the objectives we laid out on paper for ourselves ten or fifteen years earlier, but in so doing we've neglected to revise our life plans along the way. So there we are. All dressed up and nowhere to go, as the old joke has it.

That used-book business you've been spending sixteen hours a day at for so long now, miracle of miracles, runs by itself. You've got collectors calling up from as far away as Australia to bid on your first edition of Gertrude Stein, your complete set of Donald Duck comics. Your assistants can take care of just about any order. There's nothing much for you to do but sit back and read the mail—and wonder whether this was all worth waiting for. And, of course, it isn't—for it's not the achievement so much as the race itself that gives life its zest. Thus, it's important that our goals not only be realistic, but that they reflect the person we are now. Maybe (let's hope) you've changed in the last ten or fifteen years. Maybe you're really not so keen on used books anymore. It may be time to sell and move on, or expand into a related field. The important thing, though, is not what you do, but that you have enough perspective on your Crazy Me to realize that you are suffering from a form of expectational boredom and that it's time to do *something.*

Crazy Me-isms

As we've seen in this chapter, the Crazy Me is responsible for many of our bouts with boredom. Because the Crazy Me is inside, an integral part of our personalities, besting him or her is like fighting a guerrilla war. If you're going to win you've got to first learn to recognize the enemy. You can do this by listening to the kinds of statements the Crazy Me likes to make as well as by paying attention to how bad you feel when you act on his or her advice. Here are just a few of the things you're likely to overhear:

"I have to conform."

"I should be right."

"I shouldn't offend anyone."

"I shouldn't be selfish."

"I shouldn't change my mind."

"Other people know better than me."

"I should never do things without a good reason."

"Indecisiveness is a sign of weakness."

"I shouldn't admit my mistakes."

"I should be very careful not to take chances where I might get hurt."

"My life should be free of conflict."

107

"There is a clear right and wrong."

"I'm not very lucky."

"I have no control over what happens to me."

"Everything I do is equally important."

"Life should be taken seriously."

"If I only had [a million dollars, a child, a job, a guitar, someone to love, etc.] then I'd be happy."

"I should always think through the consequences of my actions."

"I should finish what I start."

Fortunately, we don't have to take all this propaganda lying down. We have an ally in the struggle for a more rewarding existence. Our Sane Me is waiting in the wings.

4 *Getting to Know the Sane Me*

Enter the Sane Me

Curious, confident, committed to change—the Sane Me adopts an experimental approach to life. You can always tell when he or she is on stage—though most likely you're so involved in what you're doing you won't have time to stop and think about it. If you did, you'd notice that once the Sane Me gets the upper hand three distinct things begin to happen:

1. You lose your sense of time.
2. You shed the self-consciousness that inhibits you from taking positive actions on your own behalf.
3. You're suddenly focused on the process of what you're doing rather than the product.

Let's look at a situation we've all been in—you've got to do something and you know it's going to bore you.

109

Up From Boredom, Down From Fear

Ralph and his Crazy Me are on their way to visit his in-laws. Already he's feeling bored, resentful that he's missing his Sunday afternoon football game, dreading his mother-in-law's new aches and pains and his father-in-law's interminable stories of when-I-was-a-boy. . . . But he has to go. He and his wife have been putting it off for weeks.

Ralph is heading for a good case of situational boredom—boredom that is directly caused by unavoidable circumstance. The ride over there seems to take forever. Ralph drums his fingers on the steering wheel, picks a fight with his wife, worries about whether he remembered to lock the front door, thinks about all the other things he "should" be doing, and generally exhibits the symptoms of someone in the grip of the Crazy Me.

The visit fully lives up to Ralph's expectations. He sits back, washed by waves of boredom, wishing he were somewhere, anywhere, else. His only source of satisfaction is the smug realization that things are every bit as bad as he thought they'd be.

The trip home is quite a different story. Ralph notices some new construction underway in an area that used to be a bird sanctuary. He and his wife discuss the possibility of doing something to keep the countryside from turning into yet another suburban sprawl. They get so involved in the conversation that they're home before they know it. Ralph suggests they treat themselves to dinner and a movie instead of watching their usual Sunday-night TV programs.

Clearly the Ralph who returned home that evening had little in common with the anxious angry person who'd left earlier that afternoon. The journey that had taken forever in one direction sped by on the way back. No longer hemmed in by the Crazy Me, Ralph could pay attention to the view, his wife, his need for outside stimulation. He'd forgotten about himself long enough to get involved—a sure sign that the Sane Me is once more at the helm.

Feelings associated with an eager, interested stance toward experience are important to remember. In this instance, Ralph had little control over when the Sane Me regained command. It was largely a matter of circumstance—the performance of an obligation he'd been dreading. Ideally, however, we should be able to bring about this state of mind at will so that when we're placed in a boring situation we can get involved in it and raise our arousal level into the comfort zone.

You can start to control your own arousal level with a little trick. The next time you're stuck in a boring situation, try simply wondering why the other people there are doing what they're doing. In other words, observe the problem, don't get involved and become part of it. Explore an area of someone's life that you don't know about—their schooldays, their politics—something you've never discussed. They'll be delighted. Or try telling them something they've never heard before about you. Everyone can be reached.

Even the most mundane situation can become interesting if you take a fresh look at it. The other day I found myself with a long, empty afternoon to fill. I'd had a couple of drinks and was ready for an adventure. I decided to approach total strangers on the street, telling them I was collecting information for a book on boredom. One of the people I stopped was a man who looked fifty but turned out to be seventy. When I asked him what bored him in life, he said, "Nothing bores me. Every experience is new if you just look carefully." And, pointing down the alleyway behind us, he exclaimed, "You see that alley? That's not just an alley. It's a place I've never seen before. Why, I could find lots of things that are new and exciting to me in just one simple alley."

In order to get in touch with the characteristics of your own Sane Me, try thinking about how you feel when you're doing something you really enjoy. Notice the next time this feeling begins to surface. What are you doing? Where are you doing it? With whom? And how did you get there in the first place—physically? mentally? emotionally? Tracing these journeys to sanity is one sure way to begin to recover your ability to live with gusto.

Boredom often begins with an attitude of hopelessness or, more accurately, helplessness. "It's all beyond me," people say, or "It's out of my hands," or "I've got no control over my life." Very occasionally these statements may be true. There is no doubt that a certain amount of calamity occurs at random, but far more often feelings of powerlessness are not true reflections of our actual circumstances. What are they? They're the Crazy Me either dragging us back into boredom or pushing us up into fear. In reality, most of the time we spend on earth *we are not victims*. We can "take control" and go forward with lives that are meaningful, rich and intensely experienced.

In Ralph's case, if his Sane Me had been in charge throughout the day—or at least around to counter the Crazy Me with some effective dialogue—he wouldn't have felt so helpless to change his circumstances. He could certainly have enjoyed the ride over as much as the ride back, and even the visit itself could have been far more interesting. We'll be learning the techniques for conquering situational as well as the other kinds of boredom, but first we need to learn to trust in the existence and power of our own sanity.

Stop–Think

How often have you been driven bananas by an advertising slogan or a jingle that your mind just can't stop repeating? There is, perhaps, nothing more diabolical, more infuriating, than waiting for "Ajax (boom-boom), the foaming cleanser" to float the dirt right down the drain for good. And each time you consciously try to stop the music it comes back louder than before. Hopeless, right? Wrong. There *is* something you can do. The late Dr. James G. Taylor came up with a therapy technique called *stop-think*. Developed for persons plagued by thoughts they felt they couldn't control, Dr. Taylor merely sat the patient down and asked him or her to let the obsessive tape recording play. Then, without warning, he yelled "Stop that!" at the top of his voice. The patient, stunned by this surprising behavior, understandably reacted by stopping the thought. And once it has been demonstrated that the thought *can* be turned off, the patient learns that it is he alone who decides what creatures may enter his mental landscape and how long they may stay. Then it becomes merely a question of practicing stopping. And this goes for more than soap commercials. The irrational fears that keep us locked into boredom are also subject to control.

Increasingly we are finding ways to master aspects of our minds and bodies that were formerly considered involuntary. Experiments in biofeedback prove that the heart rate, brain waves, blood pressure and muscle tension are all subject to conscious control. Scientists everywhere are rapidly approaching the same brave new world where nothing is immutable.

If you think of yourself as a system composed of interrelated actions, thoughts and feelings, it seems logical that a change in any one area will create change in the other two.

Very often just a small change in stopping an old thought or finding a new one can have dramatic effects. Not long ago I discovered that, through an unusual set of blunders, one of my patients had been misdiagnosed as a paranoid-schizophrenic. He'd spent most of his life drifting between hospitals, board-and-care homes, and skid row, wallowing in his own gloom. He was "unable" to do anything about his situation because he was a "paranoid schizophrenic." When I managed to convince him that it had all been a terrible mistake, the change was dramatic. No longer weighed down by an oppressive idea of himself, he was able to pick up his life again and move forward. Currently, he's doing productive work, seeking a reconciliation with his ex-wife, and enjoying the new vistas opened up by his "delabeling" experience.

Thought substitution is another technique that can be used along with stop-think to introduce change. You can practice it whenever you find yourself slipping into those negative cul-de-sacs frequented by the Crazy Me. It involves stopping the first thought, then replacing it with a positive one. Indulge in a pleasurable fantasy instead of dwelling on the gloomy side of what might happen. And don't stop to argue that it won't work, or wonder if it's really that simple. Spend your energy practicing instead.

You can also change the system by changing your actions. For example, say you're usually rather shy and diffident at cocktail parties. One night you make up your mind to say good-bye to all that. You start asking questions you've never dared to ask, and you keep asking—not because you're rude, but because you really want to know. And pretty soon you stop *feeling* shy because people are not only telling you their secrets, they're flattered by your interest. If you're not careful you'll stop *thinking* of yourself as a wallflower and the metamorphosis will be complete.

If such a drastic about-face seems impossible to accomplish without some help, let me assure you that not only can you do it, but you are never without support when it comes to moving out of the pale of your own insanity. The Sane Me is your constant companion. Even when you are at your craziest, you can always count on having "someone" to turn to who can tell you how things "really are." The Sane Me is capable of recognizing that the Crazy Me is, in fact, crazy. Consulting the Sane Me requires only that you come to trust your own perceptions of the world—to listen to what Dr. Brugh Joy calls "the inner teacher."

A patient of mine learned this only after slogging through three long years of law school. His father had convinced him to follow in his footsteps, though Ted had protested vigorously. "I hate paperwork," he'd said, "and I'm not even interested in the law. It's boring." "But look at the way you love to read detective stories, think about how you used to love to come to court with me," his father had pleaded. "Believe me, you have what it takes. Once you're in law school you'll see what a natural you are." Eventually Ted capitulated. He wanted to please his father and, in his heart of hearts, hoped he did have a real aptitude for legal matters. It wasn't until he'd completed his studies and begun to practice that he found time to sort out his true feelings. Nothing had changed: he still hated paperwork, still had no enthusiasm for the law. He was deeply bored. His initial reaction had been correct; Ted had simply lost heart. He failed to remain loyal to his own perception of himself. Now he was faced with finding his own way based on what he knew to be true. Unfortunately, he'd lost three precious years en route.

The frustration that comes from doing things we don't enjoy is at the root of much of our boredom. Often we're in that position because we've listened to well-meaning advice from others ("What you ought to be doing is . . ."

or "I'll tell you something. If I were in your shoes I'd . . .") instead of consulting the Sane Me about what we'd personally find rewarding.

Once you start to trust your own ability to perceive the world correctly you can adopt what I like to call the "experimental life style." You no longer have to take anything for granted, take anybody's word for it, take anything on faith. Taking things for granted, taking things on faith—these passive phrases are not in the vocabulary of the Sane Me. The Sane Me is active, inquisitive, willing to test the validity of its own conclusions.

Say you're interested in hang gliding. Chances are you'll run into a lot of resistance to the idea:

> "Hang gliding? Are you crazy? That's just for kids. You're forty-six years old, for Christsake." (Translation: You're too old to learn new tricks.)

> "Hang gliding? Oh, come on, Chuck, if you're out to commit suicide there are a lot easier ways than that." (Translation: Only madmen take up hang gliding; you are obviously deranged for even suggesting it.)

Rather than caving in to scare tactics based on other's fears, the Sane Me will examine the facts and come to a decision based on the risks involved and the strength of his or her desire to try it. The Sane Me is responsible, rational, independent, open, risk-taking, pragmatic, disciplined, confident and self-accepting.

Now that you know you've got an ally in your struggle with the Crazy Me, let's try it out in one of the areas that's most susceptible to boredom—relationships. What could be more tragic than the erosion that typifies human interactions? We meet and we are attracted to one another's ideas, characters, bodies, interests, styles, areas of special knowledge. Maybe we only share a few weeks together, or maybe it's for fifty years, but the excitement of the first "close encounter" is usually short-lived. Relationship boredom soon intervenes. Whole lives are spent wondering what went wrong, or trying to reenact the past, or blaming one another for not fulfilling the promise of those early days. The ability to keep the spark of love alive is rare indeed. But we all have it. It's there—if we have the courage to trust our own hard-won convictions.

My friends Tom and Janice saved their marriage from relationship boredom by ignoring just about everybody's advice. Tom, a geologist fresh out of graduate school, had been offered a job in a remote area of the Midwest. It was a plum—just what he needed to get his career off to a good start, and he looked forward to the prospect of space and solitude after years of being cooped up in the city. Janice, however, was less than thrilled. She was quite happy in Los Angeles; she had a reputation as a promising young artist, lots of close friends, and besides, she had become a little bored with Tom as it was. "How will I feel about him if we're thrown together in the middle of nowhere?" she asked me one afternoon.

Tom encouraged Janice to talk about her misgivings, though sometimes, he said, he wished he'd married someone a little more conventional, someone who didn't have to question everything as though it had never happened to anyone else before. But he took her objections seriously, and together they worked out what seemed to be a reasonable compromise. Janice would keep her studio in L.A. and spend half the year here and half there. That way she could use the isolation to really get into her work without losing all her contacts in the city. This solution seemed far from ideal to their family and friends, however. "Are you two separating?" was the usual reaction, mixed with "It's only a matter of time before you both find someone else." In most people's minds it was almost axiomatic that an unconventional approach to this common problem would inevitably lead to disaster. To their way of thinking Janice was just being pigheaded. "Imagine, refusing to give up your career for your husband!" Very rarely did anyone comment on their resourcefulness or their courage. The plan, as it turns out, has worked just fine. Tom and Janice enjoy their time together, as well as their time apart. It's not all smooth sailing, of course, but neither their marriage nor their careers have gone stale.

People who are seldom bored—whether it's in relationships, jobs or their "spare" time—are people whose Sane Me is almost always in charge. Change is one of the few constants in their lives. Security and predictability, they've learned, lead straight to boredom. They recognize that if something does go wrong it's not the end of the world; they're capable of meeting the challenge creatively. They've put the lid on paralyzing self-criticism. They are free, and they know it.

Whatever Turns You On

We all need stimulation. But we don't all need, say, a high-speed car chase down the freeway everyday to keep our juices flowing. Some people need much less stimulation than others. Knowing whether you rank high, medium or low on the Need-for-Stimulation Scale that follows is an important part of getting to know the

Sane Me. After each of the statements, enter the number that best describes you. If a statement is *especially true* about you enter the number 5. If it is *especially false* enter the number 1, and so forth.

Need-for-Stimulation Scale

5 = especially true
4 = true
3 = neither clearly true nor false
2 = false
1 = especially false

1. I often find it difficult to relax and just do nothing. _____

2. I don't seem to be comfortable unless I have three or four things going at once.

   _____

3. I don't seem to be capable of just sitting down and watching television without doing something else at the same time.

   _____

4. I find it difficult to do the same thing for an extended period of time. _____

5. It would be very difficult for me to have a job in which I had to do the same kinds of things day after day. _____

6. I would describe myself as a tense person. _____

7. I find that I am happiest when my life is packed with all sorts of different things and I barely have time to do them all.

   _____

8. I like people who are controversial and with whom you can get into a rousing discussion. _____

9. I do different things with different friends. _____

10. I believe that I know about a greater variety of things than the average person. _____

11. A quiet evening at home listening to music is one of my favorite activities. _____

12. There is a great deal to be said for working at more than one job. _____

13. I drink alcohol or coffee, take drugs and/ or smoke cigarettes to excess sometimes. _____

14. I like running errands and get very impatient when something slows me down from my prearranged schedule. _____

15. My job takes me to many locations, so I don't have to stay in one place and wait for people to come to me. _____

16. I like doing more than one thing at a time. _____

17. Having sex with only one person over an extended period of time is difficult for me to imagine. _____

18. I find it difficult to understand how some people can be happy with menial jobs when they can do other, more challenging ones. _____

19. When I was a student I was in trouble more than an average number of times. _____

20. I enjoy undertaking work assignments in which it isn't initially clear if I can get the job done. _____

21. I would be willing to try a new drug for the experience, if there weren't some compelling reason to avoid it. _____

22. I am especially concerned about my health. _____

23. I worry about accidental physical injury.

_____

24. I would not discourage my child from buying a motorcycle. _____

25. I worry about offending people.

_____

26. I am afraid of dying. _____

27. I would like to see a radical change in government policy that would move away from our middle-of-the road position. _____

28. I am not satisfied with what I have.

_____

29. Once my level of skill in a particular hobby, job or whatever gets to a point where I am no longer improving I tend to lose interest. _____

30. I don't try to get each thing I start finished before embarking on anything new. _____

Scoring

1. Add up the number of questions you answered with a "4" or a "5."

2. If your score totals more than 9 or 10, you have a greater need for stimulation than most people, and vice versa. The number 9 should not be taken too literally, however. What's really important is not your exact score, but where you are in relationship to the cutoff number.

Interpretation

What is being measured here is the amount of stimulation you need to maintain a comfortable level of arousal.

People with a high need for stimulation are likely to be tense, to find it difficult to relax. They enjoy doing many things at the same time and need frequent changes in their environment. They are more likely to use drugs to increase their stimulation and change their consciousness than other people. They like the challenging aspects of their jobs and willingly put themselves under stress at home, work or play in their attempt to stave off boredom. They are, however, concerned about their health. Controversial people and people unlike themselves attract them.

Conversely, people with a low need for stimultion tend to be relaxed, to prefer doing one thing at a time, to be more likely to stay in one place. They may prefer to avoid stressful situations—jobs and people they're not sure they can cope with—in favor of the known, the familiar.

Knowing how much stimulation you need to keep you in a comfortable state of arousal can provide valuable information on how to attack your own boredom problem. For instance, if you've discovered you have a high need for stimulation and have been at the same desk for twenty years, no wonder you're bored. If your stimulation need is not so high and you've got a job that keeps you constantly

on the go, you may be suffering from stress-symptom boredom—the boredom that comes from being overstimulated
for so long that you're jaded. Nothing excites you anymore. Look over your answers to the statements on the
Need-for-Stimulation Scale for clues as to where you might
look for ways to bring the amount of stimulation you're
getting more in line with the amount of stimulation you
need.

Keep in mind, though, that while we differ in the overall
level of stimulation we require, we all need different
amounts of stimulation at different times. Even the highest
sensation seekers find they have a yen for occasional moments of peace and quiet—if only to provide a change!
While the more serene, contemplative person can often do
with a bit of stress, lest he find himself settling into a dull
and unchallenging routine.

We also differ in terms of the activities we find exciting.
One man's meat is, indeed, another's poison. Reading, for
instance. Some people crave the written word as others
yearn for chocolate ice cream—not that the two are mutually exclusive. Give me a good book *and* a dish of chocolate ice cream any day! Other people, however, associate
books with nothing better to do. They buy them (if at all) to
decorate their shelf space, or maybe they find them useful
for reference or information. But for pure unadulterated
enjoyment—never.

Never? Well, hardly ever. Sometimes it happens that the
activities you don't even consider as sources of stimulation
are the very ones that can lead you out of the wilderness.
The other day Susan was telling me about her mother, who
is a gardening fanatic. When she was young, she said, her
mother would drag her to nurseries and flower shows every
weekend, pointing out the latest crops of this plant and that
plant, complete with Latin names, and expecting Susan

(with whom she was very close) to share her enthusiasm. Susan tried hard, but somehow it all left her cold. "All I could think about then," she said, "were the clothes I would have bought with the money Mom had just spent on another *Ficus benjamina*." Now Susan's grown. She has her own house and garden and she's no longer so obsessed with her wardrobe. But she has developed an interest in things horticultural. More and more she and her mother find themselves talking about when to plant and how best to prune.

The moral to this story is, of course, that the things that intrigue us change with time. If we let them, that is. Very often we continue to live out an image that others have labeled us with: "Oh, that Joe, he sure does love to dance." When in fact Joe may have gotten bored with the bump or the boogaloo long ago. But he just keeps hoofing, since that's what's expected of him. He may not even know he's tired of it all, since the expectations of others play such a powerful role in our lives.

So what do you do when you need a change of pace?

Stimulation-Source Profile

To find out where your Sane Me presently looks for stimulation and to point out areas that might profit from further exploration, I've developed a Stimulation-Source Profile. Your reaction to these statements will identify you as a juicer, an egghead, a player or a goalie.

Briefly, these categories indicate where you are most likely to look for activities to increase your arousal level. Juicers turn to risk-taking, eggheads to learning, players to the process of doing itself and goalies to achieving. To clarify the differences between these personality types, we can use the analogy of how each one might function sexually. The juicer would be aroused by the riskier, even illicit, aspects of sex, while the egghead would be interested in what he was learning about himself and/or the other person. The player would be caught up in the actual process of the sex act itself, and the goalie would concern himself primarily with orgasm and its relative magnitude. All of us are part juicer, part egghead, part player and part goalie, of course. But usually one of these aspects of the Sane Me predominates. Identifying the roles they play in your makeup will familiarize you with those parts of your personality that can lift you out of the doldrums.

Enter the number that best describes you after each of the statements:

> 5 = especially true
> 4 = true
> 3 = neither true nor false
> 2 = false
> 1 = especially false

Juicers–Risk Takers

1. I enjoy gambling. _____

2. I often do things that are dangerous just for the excitement. _____

3. I enjoy being a little frightened.

   _____

4. I find heights exhilarating rather than frightening. _____

5. Life is full of dangers and I'm not sure I'd be willing to sacrifice the spice these dangers offer to make it safer. _____

6. If I had any money to invest, I would be likely to put it into stocks and commodities rather than a savings account.

   _____

7. I like trying different restaurants even if they haven't been recommended.

   _____

8. I enjoy the unpredictability inherent in traveling. _____

9. I am likely to do things on the spur of the moment without much planning.

   _____

10. I think that children are becoming too conservative these days. _____

11. I am given to impulsive buying.

    _____

12. I enjoy sexual experimentation.

    _____

13. I have fears that prevent me from acting out my fantasies. _____

14. If I am not certain whether another person would like to be with me I'm very likely to ask them to do something.

    _____

15. Frequent changes of jobs can be exciting. _____

16. I sometimes think of living in more dangerous times. _____

17. I would like to change my life style just to see what would happen. _____

18. I have shoplifted inexpensive items that I could easily have bought. _____

19. It is not hard for me to understand the

motivation of explorers and soldiers of fortune. _____

20. If I had lived in the United States in the middle 1800s I would like to think that I would have lived in the West. _____

21. I would rather trade stocks on the floor of the New York Stock Exchange than be a librarian. _____

22. I have on occasion had sexual intercourse with two or three people in a single day. _____

23. A quiet evening at home listening to music is not one of my favorite activities. _____

24. I prefer action-oriented vacations rather than resting vacations. _____

25. Getting "somewhere" in life is not as important as enjoying the trip. _____

26. Competitive forms of exercise such as baseball, basketball and tennis are more interesting than noncompetitive exercise such as bicycle riding or jogging. _____

27. Participant sports interest me since I can always improve on my performance. _____

28. People are interesting to me because they teach me something about myself. _____

29. If I were in a different foreign city I would not like to take a guided tour of some sort before exploring on my own. _____

30. As soon as I am certain how a book,

movie or play is going to end, I'd just as soon not finish it. _____

31. It is difficult for me to sit in one place for any length of time. _____

Eggheads-Learners

1. I think the educational process is one of the most rewarding human experiences.

_____

2. It is difficult for me to accept things at face value without some deeper understanding. _____

3. I find myself asking "why" more than most people. _____

4. If I were an explorer I would be more motivated by curiosity than by fame or wealth. _____

5. Documentary programs on television are more to my liking than situation comedies. _____

6. I prefer to spend time with people who don't always think the same way I do.

_____

7. When a workman comes to repair something in my home I am always interested in what he or she is doing and how the object in question works. _____

8. I think I know more about more things than the average person. _____

9. My job involves a great deal of activity so that sometimes I physically can't get

everything done that needs to be done.

    ————

10. It is easy for me to spend an evening just reading a book.

    ————

11. I enjoy going to museums.

    ————

12. If I go window shopping with some friends I am likely to lag behind.

    ————

13. I would rather listen to a lecture than engage in some participatory activity.

    ————

14. It's hard for me to understand why some people like to go dancing at a place where the music is exceptionally loud and the light shows are quite intense.

    ————

15. It is not difficult for me to maintain my interest in long-term projects.

    ————

16. I care relatively little about what people think of me.

    ————

17. At work I like to push myself to the limits rather than get into a groove and coast.

    ————

18. I eat foods I like even if they tend to disagree with me.

    ————

19. Frequent changes of jobs aren't exciting for me.

    ————

20. Unexpected events throw me off balance.

    ————

21. I don't like to indulge myself in fads and new fashions.

    ————

22. I would not be likely to mortgage my home if a good business deal turned up.

    ————

23. I tend to live in the present rather than in the future. _____

24. I have no particular interest in getting anywhere in this lifetime. _____

25. I am more interested in doing my job well than in advancing or learning another job. _____

26. I like doing one thing at a time. _____

27. My job is unpredictable in the sense that every day is different. _____

Players-Processors

1. If I am sexually interested in another person I enjoy the process of seducing them as much as, if not more than, the sexual consummation of our interaction.

    _____

2. Most of my activities are intrinsically enjoyable. _____

3. I tend to live in the present rather than the future. _____

4. I admire children who get totally involved in what they are doing. _____

5. One of the big problems that I see wrong with people is that they don't enjoy what they are doing. _____

6. I get a lot of satisfaction from doing what other people would consider simple tasks. _____

7. When I take on a job I am primarily motivated by doing what has to be done to get

the job done without considering the implications of completing or not completing it. _____

8. I generally feel that I know enough about the world to get by and I am not particularly interested in learning a lot of new things. _____

9. If I had to guess, I would say that my sexual encounters last longer than the national average. _____

10. I can see how some people would be more interested in cooking than they would be in eating. _____

11. One of the most disturbing ideas about marriage to me is that you seem to be forced to spend a great deal of time with one person. _____

12. I tend to be outspoken rather than reticent. _____

13. I am willing to speak my mind and take my chances over losing friends.

_____

14. I believe it's true that everything has a cost and that most experiences are worth the price. _____

15. If I have to make a speech before a group I prefer to "wing" it rather than plan it very carefully. _____

16. At work I tend to talk back to superiors.

_____

17. I am more ruled by my emotions than my intellect. _____

18. I enjoy getting to know new people.

_____

19. As a child I frequently took things apart to see what made them tick. _____

20. I would not like to see our government spend more money on research. _____

21. My friendships last longer than most people's. _____

22. When I take on a new leisure activity I do not formulate some plan as to what I would like to accomplish. _____

23. I like people who are controversial and with whom you can get into a rousing discussion. _____

24. I prefer resting vacations rather than action vacations. _____

25. I would like to see a radical change in government policy that would move away from our middle-of-the-road position. _____

26. It is easy for me to accept things at face value. _____

27. If I were in a different foreign city I would not take a guided tour of some sort before exploring on my own. _____

28. I am not satisfied with the amount of income that I have. _____

29. I tend to live in the present and enjoy today. _____

Goalies-Achievers

1. Without goals I doubt if I would do many of the things I do now. _____

2. My primary motivation in sex is to have an orgasm. _____

3. I tend to look at life in terms of seeing how far I can go. _____

4. Materialistic things are quite important to me. _____

5. I would like my children to get somewhere in life. _____

6. I tend to look down the road and make plans for the future, rather than living in the present and enjoying today.

   _____

7. I have a pretty good idea of what I would like to be doing at work next year.

   _____

8. I can visualize what my next residence would look like if I could have my way.

   _____

9. I enjoy planning for the future.

   _____

10. I don't believe in living in the present and letting the future take care of itself.

    _____

11. People who talk slowly seem to bore me a great deal. _____

12. Unless a movie has a great deal of action in it I usually don't enjoy it. _____

13. If I were to go swimming at the beach I would not be likely to take along some games, books and other "diversions" to keep me occupied. _____

14. When I was in school I liked it better when the semester was busy than when the semester was quiet. _____

15. I would rather be assigned a difficult task at work than one that is blatantly simple.

_____

16. I often seem to have a lot of excess energy to work off. _____

17. It is difficult for me to linger at meals and I generally finish before most of my friends. _____

18. I think waiting in line is more difficult for me than for the average person.

_____

19. I worry too much about being economically secure when I retire. _____

20. I have started, or think I would find it exciting to start, my own business.

_____

21. I enjoy working around my house, fixing it up and taking care of it. _____

22. I don't agree with the statement "It's not whether you win or lose but how you play the game." _____

23. If I were to move to a new city I would enjoy looking for a place to live.

_____

24. I am interested in getting somewhere in this life. _____

25. I am not curious about what it would have been like to live in the past.

_____

Scoring

1. Add up the number of questions in each category that you answered with a "4" or a "5."

2. If your score is 13 or more in the juicer category, risk-taking is probably a significant source of stimulation for you. A score of 11 or more on the egghead section indicates that much of your stimulation comes from learning. Nine or more in the third category shows that the process itself is very important for you. And if you got 9 or more in the last section you get much of your satisfaction from goal-oriented activity.

The actual numbers are not nearly as important as the relationship of one score to another. For it is this mix—the particular way that these aspects of your own personality meld—that will give you a sense of where you look now for stimulation, and will provide clues to other areas that might bring you up from boredom.

You may find that you score high in more than one category. That's fine. The categories are not necessarily mutually exclusive. Although my research indicates that these factors are not *necessarily* connected to one another, in your case they may be. Don't worry about it. If you're both a juicer and a goalie, for instance, you'll have twice as many options when you're looking for sources of additional stimulation in your environment. Low scores point to a style of getting stimulation that you are probably overlooking.

Interpretation

In developing the Stimulation-Source Profile I came up with a very clear picture of the general characteristics of each of these personality types. We'll examine them in more detail, but first of all, let me clarify one thing. These categories have nothing to do with *how much* stimulation you need. People with high, medium and low needs for sensation are found in all categories. Nor do they refer to *what* you do. A mountain-climber, for instance, might be up there for the risks involved, the learning experience, the climb itself or the achievement of getting to the top.

The Juicer

Let's look first at the juicer. He thrills to the danger of it all, the lure of the unknown. You might find him on the floor of the stock exchange, stomping around on the dark side of the moon or challenging the establishment from behind a barricade. For the juicer, living dangerously is a full-time job. Both his or her personal and professional life are likely to reflect a taste for skimming the abyss, a fascination with "what ifs," a commitment to trying every-thing at least once just to find out what it's like. The uncer-tainties of life—whether they're found in business, sports or intellectual activities—are his meat and drink.

Frankie is a perfect example. He's a businessman, but not your steady, stolid Chamber of Commerce variety. Frankie is more of an entrepreneur, a hustler, if you will, who likes to be in on the ground floor of things. If it's new, far out, a long shot, a gimmick no one's ever heard of (much less think they need) that's Frankie's ballpark. Hot tubs, Cuisinarts, Beta Max—they're all old hat to him. Eternally on the lookout for something new to back, right now he's into home computers. And he'll probably make a bundle. Because he's more interested in taking chances than in reaping vast profits, his business ventures seem doomed to succeed. But even if he fails, Frankie will bounce back, ready to lay it all on the line again at the first opportunity that comes his way. Why does he run around all day like a maniac? Why not settle for a plain, ordinary,

136

nine-to-five ulcer-free job? It's too easy, he'll tell you. It's the one thing guaranteed to drive him up the wall with boredom is what he means. He's just not cut out for it.

Acting on impulse, taking the "road less traveled by," juicers try to avoid the safety of the known, the too familiar. Action addicts, they opt for participation rather than observation. Juicers who find themselves stuck in jobs or life styles with a high degree of predictability either need to find ways to introduce an element of risk into their circumstances or change the circumstance itself. There's a delicate balance, however, between the excitement of living dangerously and the fear that comes with overarousal. Learning to take "enough" chances to bring you up from boredom without crossing the border into fear is the tightrope act each juicer must eventually learn to master.

The Egghead

The next category, the egghead, is my own particular area of expertise. And by egghead I don't necessarily mean an intellectual. An egghead could just as easily be a car mechanic who likes to work on unfamiliar makes and models to find out how they tick. An egghead is a student—someone more interested in learning *how* to do something than in actually doing it. And they are not as common in academia as you might assume. Some professors are there for the status and the tenure (goalies), others because they like the very process of teaching and research (players), and still others because they enjoy introducing innovative programs and challenging the status quo (juicers). It is a minority who are there because they really like to learn. The same goes for college students. Most want their degrees, their careers—and the classes they need to

137

get them are merely hurdles to be cleared on the way. Nor are eggheads necessarily shy and retiring. Their area of interest might well be in learning about other people.

Eggheads have a strong need to understand the world, a curiosity about how it all works. Often you can tell them by the way they talk about themselves. They're likely to have a hard time describing what they do because they can do so many things. "I'm a jack of all trades, master of none." Our culture imbues us with the idea that there's something wrong with this stance toward life. If you're not committed irrevocably to one course of action, then you're not really *serious*. And the frivolous person is not to be trusted—perhaps because he's likely to have fun, which, according to Calvin, leads inexorably to divine retribution!

I often meet with disbelief when my various colleagues discover that I'm not just a professor, a practicing psychologist, a backgammon player, or an author, but a bit of each. Usually the assumption is that if you do more than one thing you must not be much good at any of them. The exceptions to this "rule" are numerous enough to make it highly suspect. Although I can hardly claim kinship with the likes of Leonardo, look at just a few of those who've refused to be bound by narrow and arbitrary definitions of themselves—Leonardo da Vinci, George Bernard Shaw, Bertrand Russell, Eric Hoffer, Albert Schweitzer, Ronald Reagan, Billy Carter—from the sublime to the ridiculous. And the list could go on and on. The fact is that there is a little of all of the spirit of these people in every one of us—if we're ingenious enough to find it.

In many ways learners epitomize the most positive aspects of the "laid-back" life style that's become something of a popular ideal among the young. They're not rushing to make the next train and they have little need for frequent change in their lives. Neither dwelling in the past nor living for the future, they're content with a life of quiet investigation and contemplation of whatever they're learning in the present. The danger is, of course, that things will get too quiet. It's especially important for eggheads to examine their feelings, thoughts and actions frequently for signs of boredom, because people with life styles that do not automatically incorporate the stimulation of constant change may need to think of ways to include it consciously. Besides, they might just learn something!

The Player

Our third category is the player—the person who lives for the doing of the thing itself. This point of view is much beloved in Eastern philosophy, but not so popular in the West. Here, until recently, one jogged to get to the finish line, not for the "zen of running." But there have always been those who didn't much care about whether they won or lost, only how they played the game. The opportunity to participate, the reality of simply playing the game itself, is of utmost importance to the player, and is a way to reduce boredom.

Take my colleague, Jane. She loves to write textbooks. She already knows the subjects, so it's not the challenge of learning something new that intrigues her. She takes few risks and professes little ambition. What she *does* love is solving the technical and organizational problems involved in putting information together in an intelligent, readable form.

Then there's my wife, Karen. She spent the other day at her loom, weaving from morning till night. When the piece was finished it looked atrocious. How can I spend the whole day making something so ugly and not feel concerned about it, she wondered. The answer, of course, was that she thoroughly enjoyed the process, even though the product was not at all what she had in mind.

Players tend to live very much in the present, to be process-oriented and indifferent to the lure of success. Their involvement in actions rather than consequences frees them to live rather impulsively. Often they are very outspoken and tend to be ruled more by emotion than intellect. Life is accepted and enjoyed at face value. Its rewards are those of "seizing the moment."

In their fascination with the trees, however, the player may lose sight of the forest. His or her life can drift into boredom due to a lack of goals or an unwillingness to stand back and look at the whole picture. Players can often benefit from occasionally putting themselves in the shoes of a goalie.

The Goalie

A goalie is in many respects the quintessential American. Materialistic and achievement-oriented, he is driven to succeed. Invariably he looks for the product, the answer, the bottom line in whatever he does. Forever restless, he wants to get on with it—to "get there," whether "there" is the top of the heap or the end of the rainbow. If he has a major fault, it is his penchant for being too far out in front of himself. Living mostly in the future, the goalie finds it hard to enjoy the present, to engage in activities that have no definite purpose or end result.

Like juicers, eggheads and players, goalies pop up in all

walks of life. They're not just football coaches or civil engineers. But they all live fast-paced lives, expending a lot of nervous energy along the way. Winning is important to them and they are therefore adept at keeping score. Some are dreamers and poets as well. They are all planners and, as such, are deeply committed to their own particular futures. And this is as it should be, for goalies are fueled by desire. As Bette Davis put it recently, "The exciting part of the work is the challenge to get there."

Walter is determined to make a million dollars by the time he's fifty. And he's well on his way to doing it. But at a price. The other aspects of Walter's life—his wife and family, his fondness for Bach, even physical comfort and good health—are overshadowed by the dedication with which he pursues his pot of gold. He works as a commodities broker and gambles on the side—sounds like a juicer, right?—but he only buys or bets when he's absolutely sure all the odds are in his favor. He keeps meticulous records, works like a dog and puts up with a lot of mundane annoyances—all in honor of an idea he conceived as a child of twelve. "I promised myself I'd die a millionaire," he confided when we first met. But not long after that Walter changed his mind. He realized he didn't want to wait that long, and set fifty as a more desirable goal. I often wonder, though, what he'll do when he makes it. Most likely he'll just raise his sights and keep on doing what he's always done. For Walter, like many goalies, may find himself floundering once he actually gets there. He's neglected to create a life for himself in the present, so when he achieves his goal there'll be nothing much left to live for. If Walter is smart (and he is), he'll begin to make contingency plans now, so that when he's rolling in clover he'll have something besides money to give meaning to his life.

141

Up From Boredom, Down From Fear

Knowing your own leaning, whether you're a juicer, egg-head, player or goalie, is not only useful as an indicator of where to look for stimulation when you're bored, it's also an excellent guide to those areas you may have been neg-lecting. The person who sees himself as a juicer may con-tinually turn to more and more adventure as the *only* way out of boredom. He grows jaded—habituated to a stimula-tion level impossible to sustain. He may do well to consult the other faces of the Sane Me, take time out perhaps to exercise the goalie or the player in him. Similarly, even the most dedicated egghead will tire of endless learning, and benefit from inquiring into the pleasures of juicing, the thrills of achievement.

When I was in college, I met a young physicist who was worried that all the important discoveries in his field had al-ready been made. "There'll be nothing left for me to do," he complained, "but teach the same old stuff year after year." His fears were, of course, unfounded. Since that time physicists have made astounding breakthroughs—the laser, the quark, the tachyon. This fear that the world is go-ing to let you down, that there are no surprises anymore (at least not pleasant ones) leads straight to boredom.

The fact is that the world is a very generous place, full of wonder, novelty and endless sources of stimulation. If our Sane Me is open, daring and strong enough to challenge our "crazy" thoughts, feelings and actions, there's nothing to prevent us from seizing and savoring all the opportunities for meaningful involvement that come our way.

Just to remind ourselves of what the Sane Me sounds like, here's a list of the kinds of statements you're likely to hear when "all's right with the world." Even though some of the things on this list may sound a little crazy to you at first, let me assure you that they're not. . . .

I may choose to, but I don't have to, conform.

It's okay to make mistakes.

There are times when people will be offended by my behavior.

There is nothing wrong with being interested in myself.

I'm not such an awful person.

It's okay to change my mind.

My opinion is just as good as someone else's.

I don't always have to have a good reason for doing something.

Taking chances and losing is part of life.

Conflict is part of life.

No one thing will ever bring me complete and lasting happiness.

There often is not a clear right or wrong.

Not everything I do is serious.

I don't have to finish what I start.

My life may never be neat and orderly with no loose ends.

People often have more important things to do than evaluate my behavior.

I don't have to prove myself.

I am neither totally innocent nor totally guilty.

The world is not to blame for my problems.

I have power.

Up From Boredom, Down From Fear

I don't need everyone's love.

It is okay to indulge myself.

It won't do me any good to worry about things that are out of my control.

There is no way to eliminate all risks.

The question that remains, of course, is why we don't think, feel and act like this all the time.

5 *Stuck in the Mud;*
Why We Stay Bored

FEIFFER BY JULES FEIFFER

The chief culprits in the plot to snuff out our
hero, the Sane Me, are those two villains we've met briefly
already, the Prosecuting Attorney and the Prophet of
Doom. We're going to learn how to put them in their place,

but first we need to make sure we know exactly who they are, where they come from, and why they're so hard to shake. You'll recognize them, I'm sure. . . .

The Prosecuting Attorney and the Prophet of Doom

The Prosecuting Attorney, or the resident critic, as Feiffer calls him, keeps you in line by continually making you feel guilty for not doing what you "should." At the slightest sign of activity on your part, the Prosecuting Attorney is there to tell you (a) you're doing it wrong, (b) you have no right, (c) there's something wrong with you for wanting to do it, or (d) you should be doing something else. The inevitable result of this constant carping is that you end up adopting the Prosecuting Attorney's values as your own—values that lead to boredom every time. You're either doing things you don't want to do but think you should, or doing nothing at all.

The Prosecuting Attorney is perpetually on the attack. He figures that if he can make you feel bad enough about yourself then you'll try to atone for your sins by following the Prosecuting Attorney's orders. And this whole process starts very early in life. A preschool teacher I know was shocked to find that when she asked her class of seemingly confident, happy four-year-olds to tell her what they liked about themselves, no one could think of anything to say. A sunny, freckled little girl finally burst out: "I don't like myself. I hate myself!" The rest of the children then chimed in with all the various things they'd learned to criticize in themselves. It's taken their teacher several weeks to con-

146

vince them that it's okay to talk about themselves as lovable people with many wonderful qualities. And then there's this example of self-criticism produced by a seven-year-old friend of mine.

1. I ma Fat.
2 I waht to be all. ⌐ I want to
3 I eat to much 7 I bant want to
   sugar.   get in to a
                       foght.
4 I want to be 8 I
   skinny.
5 I Yell at my
   mam.
6 I hate my sell

Much of the Prosecuting Attorney's power over you lies in the universal tendency to take his presence for granted. Once you recognize that he's there, however, and that he's holding you back, you can begin to reclaim the power to direct your life.

One of my patients, Nancy, has been suffering from periodic bouts of severe expectational boredom for a very long time. Her boredom is high aspiration-induced and is

147

brought on by an unusually harsh Prosecuting Attorney who sets very high standards for her, always choosing objectives that are nearly impossible to achieve. Nancy is a very bright, competent young woman, however, and usually manages to come pretty close to her target. Take her job. She's a publicist for one of the big record companies in town. When she started working there she told me she'd be second in command by the end of the year. And she just about made it. Her promotion was announced last February. By that time, though, her achievement was no longer a source of satisfaction. Nancy's Prosecuting Attorney had raised the ante on her. "Stop kidding around, Nancy," he told her in effect. "You're sharper than any six of these clowns put together. You know very well that you should be the *director* of public relations." And this is how it goes. . . . Each time Nancy approaches success, it is snatched away from her by an insatiable Prosecuting Attorney. When things reach an impasse and she can't satisfy that last "should," Nancy disappoints herself. Her Prosecuting Attorney starts to criticize, building a case to convince her that she's worthless, citing the evidence of her inadequacy, until she feels like such a failure that all her past accomplishments seem meaningless and she starts to sink deeper and deeper into boredom. This time, though, once Nancy recognized where this negativity was coming from, she was able to distinguish between her very real triumph and the unrealistic expectations of her Prosecuting Attorney.

Not all Prosecuting Attorneys, of course, are as hungry as Nancy's. But even the least ravenous is still full of those oughts, shoulds and musts that drive us farther and farther into a dutiful, trivial and anxious existence. Fortunately, for Nancy and all the rest of us, we can learn to check our tendency toward paralyzing self-criticism by calling on the resources of the Sane Me.

Much of the Prosecuting Attorney's power lies in his or her ability to produce guilt—admittedly a strong emotion in view of all the years and years of childhood conditioning. But guilt alone is not sufficient. We are inherently playful, curious creatures, capable of besting these "civilizing" overlayers—were it not for the presence of a more primitive emotion: fear. Fear is the enforcer, the heavy, the scar-face who does the Prosecuting Attorney's dirty work. In my cast of characters he's called the Prophet of Doom.

The Prophet of Doom specializes in conditional fear statements like "What if . . . ," "You'll be sorry if . . . ," "Don't come running to me if . . . ," "What would happen if . . . ?" Let's say you and your spouse have been planning an evening out for a very long time. You've made reservations, got the tickets and just as you're stepping into your new outfit the babysitter calls. She can't make it, and there's no time to get anyone else. Now the babysitter was mostly a precautionary measure. Your children are probably old enough to take care of themselves. Your friends' children, after all, have been on their own at night for some time now. So you vanquish your Prosecuting Attorney, who's accusing you of selfish, irresponsible behavior, and go.

The problem is you're not alone. All through dinner you've been listening to your Prophet of Doom wondering if the house is on fire, what would happen if one of them got sick, what if you had an accident, and so on. It's easy to tick these statements off one by one as having some possibility but only minimal statistical probability once you become aware of them. But often they've gotten so deeply internalized that they just play on and on in our heads like a broken record, limiting our actions even though barely audible to the conscious mind. So when your husband says something reassuring like "I'm sure the children will be just fine," you respond by saying "Let's skip the theater tonight. I know I'm not going to enjoy it anyway. I'm just too worried about the kids. . . ." When the Prophet of Doom wins out, it's almost always at the expense of your own needs for stimulation and involvement. Listening to and believing in the reality of these fears can become so habitual that they can run your life without your conscious knowledge.

Linda came to see me because, although she'd made up her mind to leave her husband, she just couldn't seem to walk out the door. And she didn't know why. She was bored with her marriage. She wanted to make a new start. And she'd given her decision a lot of careful thought. But when it came to actually doing something about it, she froze. When we got to the bottom of her dilemma, there was the Prophet of Doom, paralyzing her with fears like these: "What if I'm making a mistake?" "If Walter doesn't love me anymore, what makes me think anyone else will?" "What if I'm just not capable of making it on my own?" "Maybe life without Walter will be even worse than life with him." Unchallenged, these fears not only persist, they tend to multiply. We lose touch with our strengths; we forget that we are all equipped to cope with change; and our self-confidence goes right out the window. Thus we tend to remain in relationships that have long ago gone sour, jobs that fail to reward or satisfy, life styles that are totally predictable and dull. Ultimately, boredom based on fear and self-criticism becomes a life style. We change nothing, make no waves, take no chances, create no trouble.

150

The Prosecuting Attorney and the Prophet of Doom: A Show of Strength

To give you some idea of just how strong your own Prosecuting Attorney and Prophet of Doom are, I've come up with a quiz that will help you evaluate the areas in your own life where guilt, anxiety, self-criticism and fear are likely to overwhelm the voice of the Sane Me.

As in the other quizzes, enter the number that best describes your reaction to each of the following statements:

> 5 = especially true
>
> 4 = true
>
> 3 = neither true nor false
>
> 2 = false
>
> 1 = especially false

The Prosecuting Attorney

1. I don't think enough about pleasing myself. _____

2. If I know someone needs a favor, I feel compelled to offer my services. _____

3. I frequently berate myself for not being sensitive enough to other people's feelings. _____

4. It is difficult for me to accept compliments. _____

5. I feel awkward accepting presents. _____

6. I believe that self-criticism has far more positive effects than negative ones.

   _____

7. I would prefer to work for a salary rather than a commission.   _____

8. I am afraid of not doing things in the best possible way.   _____

9. I am frightened of being alone.

   _____

10. I'm more likely to think about things that could go wrong than about things that could go right.   _____

11. I am more of a pessimist than an optimist.   _____

12. I often find myself caught between two threatening outcomes (a rock and a hard place).   _____

13. I am very unlikely to shoplift anything.

   _____

14. I can do more to improve myself.

   _____

15. I should not have worked so hard when I was in high school.   _____

16. I am very sensitive to rejection.

   _____

17. I lose my temper much more than I should.   _____

18. I think everyone should be prepared to account for his or her behavior.

   _____

19. I shouldn't slough off so much at work.

   _____

20. I should use far more discipline in taking care of my body. _____

21. I have some rather severe character flaws. _____

22. I should be more concerned with my appearance. _____

·23. I have difficulty saying no to friends and neighbors who ask for charitable contributions. _____

The Prophet of Doom

1. It is difficult for me to tell a friend that I don't like something he or she has purchased. _____

2. I have trouble turning down invitations from people I don't enjoy. _____

3. I am afraid to ask for a raise because the boss might think I'm not worth it.

_____

4. It is difficult for me to push for what I want in a one-to-one social situation.

_____

5. I often feel that other people know what to do or say when I don't. _____

6. I ought to do more to help my fellow human beings. _____

7. I am afraid of the dark. _____

8. I don't do things that I would like to do because they are dangerous. _____

9. I suspect that if there were some way of

measuring it, I would be more fearful than the average person in my situation.

_____

10. I am afraid of taking chances. _____

11. It is difficult for me to talk to people in authority. _____

12. Speaking in front of groups makes me uncomfortable. _____

13. I am concerned about providing for myself in later years. _____

14. It is difficult for me to trust experts because I am not sure that they will do the job right. _____

15. I am not at ease when meeting new people. _____

16. I think a lot about what other people think of me. _____

17. I sometimes think that the final proof of my incompetence is just around the corner. _____

18. I am often so afraid of making the wrong decision that I do nothing at all.

_____

19. I am frequently afraid that people are criticizing me behind my back.

_____

20. If I have a bad experience in some area of my life it's unlikely that I would go back and try to do that thing again.

_____

21. I am afraid of dying. _____

22. I would be afraid to go for a walk in an unfamiliar neighborhood. _____

23. I sometimes try to be nice to people because I am afraid of the consequences of not pleasing them. _____

24. I probably don't have enough homeowner's, renter's, health, life and automobile insurance. _____

25. Either my mother or my father was more fearful than the average parent.

   _____

26. I try not to get involved in competition because I might wind up a "loser."

   _____

Scoring

1. Add up the number of questions in both categories that you answered with a "4" or a "5."
2. If your score is 8 or more in the Prosecuting Attorney's section, then you are probably quite susceptible to boredom based on self-criticism and guilt. A score of 8 or more on the Prophet of Doom section indicates that fear plays a large part in determining your actions and contributing to your boredom.

Interpretation

   People with an exceptionally strong Prosecuting Attorney are, overall, their own worst enemies. They are prone to self-criticism in a multitude of areas. They are dissatisfied with their looks and their personalities. They consider themselves insufficiently sensitive to others and generally irresponsible. Naturally, such a negative self-assessment makes them prone to periods of depression and leaves them open, by virtue of their guilt, to manipulation by others.

One of the most interesting findings of the testing I did in this area was that, regardless of how they actually scored on this section, 95 percent of the people surveyed described themselves as "more self-critical than the average person." This gives you an idea of just how pervasive the presence of the Prosecuting Attorney is in practically all of us.

Other traits that accompany a strong Prosecuting Attorney include defensiveness, a feeling of uncertainty with regard to the existence of any personal power, and a strong tendency toward perfectionism. These people usually have unrealistically high standards, are probably often described as "overachievers," and have trouble believing anything positive that others may say or feel about them.

Those with high scores on the Prophet of Doom scale are likely to have a pessimistic view of life. They are passive rather than assertive, unsure of themselves and socially uncomfortable. Inordinately concerned with what others think of them, they are afraid to be honest, even with their close associates, for fear of rejection. The all-pervasive presence of fear in such people's lives leads them to an unrealistic appraisal of its dangers. They constantly feel as if they are "walking on thin ice," especially at work, and their daydreams tend to reflect this preoccupation with potential disaster.

Whether you scored high or low on these scales, it's important to recognize that, to some extent, we are all subject to the inner promptings of the Prosecuting Attorney and the Prophet of Doom. Now that you have some idea of the strength of their voices, go back and assess your responses

156

to the statements for information on the particular areas where self-criticism and fear may be contributing most to your boredom.

Regardless of how persistent your own particular devils are, they have not always been with you. Guilt, anxiety and fear are strangers to the very young. How, then, do they so quickly worm themselves into the very heart of our identity?

What Will the Neighbors Think?

Socialization. Not a pretty word nor an easy task. For most parents the job of bringing up baby is fraught with uncertainty, anxiety, ghosts from their own pasts and an overriding concern with "doing the right thing"—whatever that is. Any doubts they may express on this score, however, are usually overruled, if not laid to rest, by the well-meaning advice of *their* parents, their friends with children or their friends without children, for that matter. And this advice is usually on the conservative side. Not only is it more convenient for adults to have children around who are seen but not heard, it also feels safer, because it's more familiar. After all, that's the way *they* were brought up. So rather than make a mistake (God forbid!) and/or risk the disapproval of others, most parents oversocialize their children. They say "no" to them out of habit, because it's easier than having to stop and think each time. They withdraw their approval at the slightest sign of rebellion or independence. They instill fear to modify behavior.

Granted that childhood is fraught with real danger (it's an irresponsible parent who doesn't teach Jimmy not to run

157

into the street), the problem is still that these "do's" and "don'ts" of childhood are then generalized from specific instances into an all-inclusive world view. From "Don't play with your food," "Lower your voice," "Say thank you," and so forth, little Susie is likely to draw the conclusion that to act at all is to invite disapproval. Either do what you're told or, if in doubt, stand still. Psychologists call this phenomenon *inadequate discrimination learning*. The child, in other words, learns her lessons only *too* well. Rather than learning that there are times when it's polite to talk and times when it's polite to listen, the child may conclude that it's safer not to talk at all. Or to explore. Or to take risks. Otherwise people (as personified by your parents) won't like you. As a result, exploration of the world comes to a halt, the child stops growing and boredom steps in. Much, and sometimes all, of our adult life is spent trying to break out of the stultifying effects of oversocialization by arriving at our own values and acting on them.

One of my friends has a daughter, Gail, whose dilemma is typical of the conflict between a father who thinks he knows best and a daughter who is afraid to trust her own judgment and accept the consequences. For years Gail has been something of a local celebrity. At the age of seven she won the town talent show and has had a role in just about every little-theater production there since. She's a natural actress and she knows it. But to make it big she needs polish, discipline and, of course, a little luck. Gail wants to take the chance—go to acting school, work hard and hope for a break. Her father, however, is dead set against it. "Oh, the theater's okay," he admits, "if you've got nothing better to do. But it's not a life. Go to college, get your teaching credential, and then if you still want to act, at least you'll have something to fall back on."

Gail knows this is "sensible" advice (after all, she's

been hearing similar words of wisdom all her life) but she doesn't want to take it. She's sure she'd be bored with the life of an education major. This time she wants to rely on what *she* knows about herself and what's best for her. Yet her Prosecuting Attorney tells her she'll be disappointing her parents. And, if the truth be told, her Prophet of Doom has left her more than a little scared about stepping out into that cold, heartless, dog-eat-dog world. "It would be so much easier," she confided, "just to march along the path of least resistance." If Gail can say no to her Prosecuting Attorney and her Prophet of Doom, chances are she'll also find the strength to say no to her parents—for their values spring from common ground.

One of the difficulties everyone encounters when trying to eliminate their fears is that, like the protective cautions instilled in childhood, most fears contain a kernel of truth. It's true that if you drive home alone late at night someone might be waiting for you in the bushes. Might. It's true that if you invite your next-door neighbor over for a drink he or she might get the wrong idea. But usually these fears are either highly unrealistic or their consequences are exaggerated. Try asking yourself first: "How likely is this to happen?" And then: "If it does happen, can I handle it?" In the case of the prowler lurking in the bushes, statistics are on your side. There is clearly *not* someone lying in wait behind each and every shrub. In the case of the next-door neighbor, the statistics may be against you, but it's a situation that can be handled. In both cases, the risk is worth taking. A night on the town, a new friend—without such pleasures we sink into a morass of safe, predictable boredom.

Lois works for a large aerospace company with a lot of government contracts. She's been a low-level administrator for years now and is quite capable of moving up to a po-

159

sition of greater responsibility. This particular company is not noted for its farsighted personnel policies, but Washington has been putting a lot of pressure on them lately to improve their image by promoting more women. Lois is the obvious choice. But so far she's resisted. "My parents taught me at an early age that hoping for too much was bound to lead to disappointment. Be happy with what you've got, they said." Trouble is, Lois isn't happy with what she's got. She's bored. She'd like to try her skills out on something more challenging, but her Prosecuting Attorney tells her that if she wants all those headaches she's crazy, and her Prophet of Doom warns that if she gets the job she'll probably fail because she won't be able to compete with all those hard-driving men. Or, worst of all, they'll put up with her, humor her and secretly despise her because they had to have a token woman. It is true that if Lois is promoted it will be partly because she's a woman. How humiliating, Lois thinks. I have my pride, after all. But it's also true that Lois should have been promoted long ago. If she takes the job in spite of her Prosecuting Attorney and Prophet of Doom, she's likely to discover that once she's knee-deep in the reality of daily crises her nightmares will evaporate. She'll have a hard time remembering that she ever paid them any mind. But if she lets them linger, they'll grow more and more formidable. They'll be with her, tying her to that desk, for the rest of her working life. Lois, like many of us, needs a little shove. Once she starts moving nothing will stop her. But how to take that first step?

Don't Just Stand There—Do Something!

Ultimately, the paralysis that keeps so many of us stuck in place, despite the certain knowledge that we

160

don't want to be there, can only be broken by direct action.
And there is so much in our society today that discourages
action. Take television. On any given evening as many as
eighty million people are sitting in front of their nineteen-
inch, solid-state, color-corrected consoles, soaking it in.
The stale jokes, the tired musical extravaganzas, the same
talk-show guests plugging yet another book on the Ken-
nedy assassination or Watergate or UFOs, the same cops,
cowboys and spacemen chasing the same robbers, Indians
and aliens night after night after night. Why do we keep
watching?

Well, what about that special on the sex life of the wild
mountain gorilla, or the night they showed *Casablanca* and
The Treasure of the Sierra Madre back to back? That
wasn't boring, you say. Or public television. That may be
boring sometimes, but at least it's educational. True, all
true. But it's not the exceptions that concern us here. After
all, we can all turn the television *on* when there's something we actively want to see. It's turning it *off* when we're
bored that's not so easy.

TV is a habit, an addiction. It depends on inertia for its
popularity. If you could conduct a living-room poll of television viewers at, say, nine-fifteen on any given week-
night, I think you'd find that the vast majority are bored,
but aren't about to do anything about it. The phrase "bored
stiff" originates from this tendency we have to get stuck in
the very passivity that creates the discomfort in the first
place. This happens partly because we're not even aware
that we're bored! Let's assume, however, that, having read
this far, you're aware of your ennui. Where do you go from
here?

If you're like most addicts your first reaction is probably
to draw up a quick list of why you can't do anything else.
Are you really too tired? If so, why don't you just crawl
into bed? Too broke to go out on the town? Well, who said

you have to spend money to have a good time? Is it really too late to do anything else, or are you letting yourself be hemmed in by a seventeenth-century concept of time? Try thinking instead about what else you could be doing. Just three or four quick alternatives. Now choose one of these and do it. Don't spend a lot of time trying to figure out which one is best. This is a trap. You could spend the rest of the evening in your armchair mulling over your choices without ever getting any further. Just do the first thing that comes to mind that's a little out of the ordinary. It could be as simple as turning off the TV, turning on the stereo and asking your husband if he'd care to dance.

Just as television (or just about anything else) can become a habit, you can also make a habit of avoiding boredom. The more you do it the easier it gets. The first time, mind you, is going to take some doing. Some discipline. Breaking the ice is never easy. But by the second time you'll have a bit more confidence, the third time it'll start to feel familiar, and by then you'll be well on your way.

John, one of my patients, came from one of Chicago's wealthiest families, but to look at him you'd never know it. He was neat enough, and clean, but his clothes were frayed with wear, and whatever style they once possessed was a good ten years out of date. John had decided long ago that life had no meaning, money was worthless and so was he. He'd been suffering ever since from a severe case of existential boredom. His parents had convinced him that since he hadn't earned his wealth he didn't deserve it. Now those of us who have to work for every penny may tend to agree, but at least we're able to spend what we've got. John couldn't. Each time he thought about getting something he needed, his Prosecuting Attorney accused him of self-indulgence. ("What did you do to deserve more clothes, John? The ones you're wearing are perfectly all right"),

162

and his Prophet of Doom warned him of gold diggers. ("If people suspect that you're rich they'll all be after your money"). Guilty and scared, John was unable to buy anything—anything at all—that might give him the slightest pleasure. Together, however, we worked out a gradient of spending.

I didn't ask John to *believe* that he was worth spending money on, or that nothing terrible would happen if he did it, just to *act* as though these things were true. The first day he was instructed to go buy a few small things for himself at the drugstore. Shaving lotion, a magazine, a new razor— things he didn't absolutely have to have. The next day his assignment was to purchase a shirt—nothing fancy—just an ordinary, everyday cotton shirt. And we went from there to establish new behavior patterns like treating himself to a movie, buying a present for a friend or splurging on a good meal, in spite of the still very active presence of his Prosecuting Attorney and Prophet of Doom. By changing John's behavior, no matter how uncomfortable it made him initially, I was able to help him change the thoughts and feelings that had led him to act as though life were inherently meaningless and boring. Asking him to behave as though it were okay to do things that might give him pleasure or satisfaction also churned up a lot of other patterns that were preventing John from being his own person.

Each time you act to break the habits that bind you to boredom you'll get more and more information about yourself—information you can use to further liberate the real you.

One of the reasons it's so hard to take that first step is the importance we place on relaxing, on taking it easy. Let's face it, by the end of an average day, most of us have not even begun to call upon our powers of endurance, resourcefulness or intelligence. We're so careful not to overdo, to save our strength, not to work too hard, that we not only end up bored, we also forget just how able we are, given the opportunity, to come up with creative solutions to our need for stimulation.

Impulse is a great teacher but we've learned to ignore its lessons. Rather than welcoming those sudden urges, we all have to break out and do something surprising—something totally out of character—we suppress them. The need for approval, and the fear of others' disapproval, overrides our search for stimulation.

We have been led to believe that consistency of character, pleasing others, being thought well of or liked, not offending and/or creating disturbances, and predictability of response are somehow more important than living an interesting life. From society's perspective this is, of course, true. If our social institutions are to function smoothly and efficiently, then we must all agree to conduct ourselves according to certain rules and regulations. The greater good takes precedence over individual happiness. But, as with our parents, we learn this lesson too well, and after a while the scales tip the other way. Boredom, anger, alienation and despair reach such depths that each person's unhappiness starts to make waves. We act out—individually and in groups. Society begins to crack and crumble under the strain. We've reached this point in America today. The time has come to start paying attention to impulse—not as a destructive force, but as a clue to creative ways of breaking out of the impasse created by our Prosecuting Attorneys and Prophets of Doom.

Listening to and acting on those needs for more stimulation that come to us in the guise of impulse, daydreams, wishful thinking or whatever you choose to call it doesn't have to be a big deal. It does, however, require that you

164

trust in the intuition of your Sane Me, that you learn to recognize the advice of your Prosecuting Attorney and Prophet of Doom as unreliable, and that you take some *action*.

Laura, an old friend from Manhattan, had just moved into a new neighborhood. One of the reasons she'd chosen to live there was because she'd heard it was full of interesting people. People of all different ages, nationalities and professions living together. The only trouble was, Laura wasn't meeting any of them. Oh, she knew the family next door. Occasionally she said "Good morning" to the woman across the street. And the grocer no longer asked her for her driver's license every time she wrote him a check. But it looked as if it were going to take years to really get to know anyone.

Before she moved, Laura had fantasized about neighbors who would ply her with casseroles while she settled in, invite her to drop by for coffee if she got lonely, ask her to help organize the annual block party. Once she got there she found that not only was there a total absence of coffee and casseroles, but they didn't even *have* an annual block party. Laura's first impulse was to organize one herself. "How presumptuous," scoffed her Prosecuting Attorney, "you haven't even lived here six months and already you think you know it all. Besides, you've got other, more important things to do." "Probably no one would come anyway," chimed in the Prophet of Doom, "and then you'd really look foolish." So Laura bided her time, hoping that someone else would do it. Needless to say, no one did.

Now Laura could have just forgotten the whole idea, tucked it away with all the other "might have beens," those impulses never followed up on, that everyone's collected. But instead she decided to give it a try. Laura was tired of "waiting" for an interesting life. But then she faced the question of what to do next.

165

Up From Boredom, Down From Fear

Announcing to the whole neighborhood that she wanted to organize a block party was just too scary. So she started small, testing the water, so to speak, to see whether she was on the right track. She invited the grocer and his wife over for dinner and tried out the idea on them. Their enthusiasm gave her the confidence she needed to push a little harder. And before too long she was in the thick of things—she got to know everybody and the block party was a huge success. Most important of all, she'd realized that if she chose to she could *act* on her own behalf. She was no longer the victim of her own boredom, but the agent of her own satisfaction.

Starting small is one of the ways to make sure you get started at all. If Laura hadn't taken a few preliminary steps, chances are she would never have done anything. It would have just looked like too much work. But once she did something, the plan developed a momentum of its own that carried her along with it. So if the disparity between your daydreams and reality seems to be so great that "never the twain shall meet," try getting your feet wet by settling for a little less the first time. Less is more than sitting in front of the TV night after night, right? Say your fantasy involves winning an Oscar for best actor. Rather than going for an all or nothing approach, how about trying out for the next little-theater production in town?

Getting into the habit of examining your fantasies with greater care requires some doing, especially after years of repression, sublimation and taken-for-granted frustration. But you might begin by making a list of ideas that have occurred to you in the past few weeks—impulses you dismissed or failed to follow up on. This should provide you with a whole raft of material to make your life *instantly* more engrossing. *If* you take the appropriate action, of course. For recognizing the impulse is only half the battle.

Stuck in the Mud; Why We Stay Bored

We've made the acquaintance of the Prosecuting Attorney and the Prophet of Doom, and we know the importance of contradicting their advice with direct action. Knowing that they're there is a major step forward, but ultimately it will not be enough to break their hold on your life. To get from knowledge to action you need some assistance. I've found it in the form of an ancient technique that can be traced all the way back to Moses. It's called talking to yourself.

6 Talking to Your "Self"

Old people muttering confidences into their shopping bags, children solemnly discussing the issues of the day with imaginary friends, Aunt Blanche deep in conversation with her cats—is this the stuff of madness? We've all heard the joke that it's okay to talk to yourself, but when you answer back you'd better start worrying. I say when you start answering back you're well on your way out of boredom, for it is then that the Sane Me takes the helm. And this is exactly what I propose to teach you how to do: how to talk back to your Crazy Me; how to put the Prosecuting Attorney and the Prophet of Doom in their place; how to abandon the fears of childhood while recovering its zest.

There is, in point of fact, a venerable tradition of famous men and women who regularly communed with themselves. Moses. Jesus. Mohammed. Confucius. Gautama Buddha. Joan of Arc. People who needed to be alone. People for whom the solitude in which to hear the sanity of their own voices was so important they went to extraordinary lengths to ensure it, often disappearing into the wilderness for days and weeks at a stretch.

These "pilgrimages to the self" were an accepted feature of life up until the modern era. One might argue, of course, that this was largely the result of a God-conscious world, a world blissfully ignorant of science and so, perhaps, more receptive to extra-logical phenomena: voices, visions, premonitions, and so on. But it is equally possible that the ability to communicate with oneself stemmed from the bullock-cart pace of the times, that it is easier to integrate one's "selves" when life is simpler and the pace less frenetic. Even today, in places like India and among remote tribes along the Amazon, where the continuum has been preserved intact, the seeking of the self is as natural as walking to the well for water. Indeed, the two acts are not dissimilar.

Boredom can prevail only if the Crazy Me is allowed to take and keep the offensive. Returning the Sane Me to its rightful position of power means learning when to suspect that the Crazy Me needs a talking to, and how to go about setting up a dialogue with yourself.

The boredom indicators listed back in the first chapter are always helpful clues to the presence of the Crazy Me. Briefly, if you're having trouble concentrating, feel empty, listless, uninvolved in the present moment, you have all the emotional indicators of boredom. Behavioral indicators include undirected nervous agitation, highly repetitive activities—chain-smoking, fidgeting and the like—and a lack of goal direction (doing several things at once and not paying attention to any of them). The cognitive indicators are a sense of mental confusion and uncertainty about what you'd rather be doing.

170

Once you have reason to suspect that the Crazy Me is in ascendance, you can start listening carefully to the messages he or she is giving you. Each of us has a characteristic pattern to our craziness, and identifying the particular way in which you "go crazy"—the trigger words and phrases that drive you deeper into boredom or fear—will give you the information you need to start responding to the voices of your personal Prosecuting Attorney or Prophet of Doom.

Often the mental habits that seal you into boredom are embodied in those dogmatic old saws that pass as "good advice." We hear them over and over until they become so much a part of our thinking we no longer question them. Learning to recognize when these key phrases–or dead giveaways, as I've called them—are running your life will put your Sane Me back in the driver's seat. Then you're in a position to contradict the crazy statement with a sane one, to make decisions and to take action against your own boredom.

Dead Giveaways

1. Winning Isn't Everything—It's the Only Thing: The Vince Lombardi Fallacy

On your mark, get set, go! From our earliest days in the schoolyard, through Little League and Homecoming Queen, to the race for that next promotion, we're encouraged to compete. Competition is a great motivator, but it can also blind us to the pleasures of process. When our eyes are too firmly fixed on the finish line, we forget to enjoy the running itself. This is not to say that winning isn't

171

fun. But win or lose, if you've enjoyed playing the game, you come out far, far ahead. So it's important to figure out ways of reaching for your objective that will be pleasurable in themselves. And this goes for everything—from playing marbles to playing the stock market.

Bob is an avid environmentalist. He's also something of a recluse. When his rather remote part of the country was chosen as a potential site for a nuclear power plant he was not only outraged, he took it as a personal affront. He decided to run for public office on the strength of his convictions alone—not because he looked forward to campaigning or holding office. He just wanted to win the election so he could stop that power plant. Through all the backslapping, handshaking and baby kissing, Bob was miserably bored. His lack of enthusiasm was contagious and he lost. Now losing per se is no big deal, if only he'd enjoyed the campaign itself. And what about the nuclear power plant?

Bob took some time out to think things over afterward. He decided to try another tack. One of the things he enjoys most is walking through the woods, observing wildlife. He started noting down the changes that would take place there if the plant went through. Eventually these notes grew into articles. The local paper published some of them and they've stirred up quite a controversy. Bob is far more effective as a naturalist and reporter than a political campaigner, and public opinion seems to be swinging his way. But even if the power plant wins in the end, Bob will not feel he's wasted his time doing something that he found intellectually boring.

Closely related to the Vince Lombardi Fallacy is the notion that you've got to be the best at everything you do—that if you don't have the talent to be a concert pianist, or the reflexes of a top athlete, there's no point in playing the piano or indulging in sports. Regardless of what our par-

172

ents told us we are not all going to be President of the United States, nor are we all destined for fame and fortune. But our lives can still be brimming with delight.

Another notion that brings us down is the belief that a talent or skill that goes unrecognized is somehow lost. A friend of mine who's a very fine but unknown painter just up and quit one day. The thought of all that work piling up in her studio was too depressing, she said. She's still depressed, but now she's also bored because she doesn't even have her painting to look forward to. Stories we hear about artists and composers whose greatness went unnoticed during their lifetime imply that their lives would have been happier had they been famous. This may be true—they would certainly have eaten better—but what goes unsaid is that the rewards of doing good creative work are considerable in themselves.

Another corollary to the Vince Lombardi Fallacy is the fear of failure that haunts us all. We're all human, yet the quest for perfection is so pervasive that we don't even allow ourselves a small mistake now and then, as though to err automatically makes us worthless. Not exactly an attitude to foster a more freewheeling approach.

The nice thing about life is that it's not like school. In school if you receive an F you've "failed"—there's no doubt about it. In real life "failure" means nothing more than a temporary reversal of fortunes. The game continues. So if you've failed at something you thought you wanted to do, try again. Or try something new. So what if you don't succeed? The only real loss is having no new game, goal or activity. It is the tendency to view one isolated failure as reason to give up that prevents good ideas from coming to fruition.

Deborah had married young. It was a disaster. Both she and her husband were naive about money, about sex and

173

about the difficulties of learning to live with another person. When they separated after ten tempestuous months, Deborah found herself deeply in debt, convinced she was frigid, and a committed spinster. Never again, she vowed. Now, some fifteen years later, Deborah is an established writer of children's books. She lives alone and is really quite content with her life, but she finds all the men she meets very dull. Deborah is afraid. She doesn't want to repeat her early mistake, so her "encounters" with men are just that—encounters, superficial relationships of convenience. There is no room set aside for intimacy or growth. What Deborah doesn't realize is that her own fears are responsible for her relationship boredom. The men who might provide her with more stimulation are automatically rejected as a potential threat, or reduced to a common denominator; they are labeled to fit more easily into Deborah's black-and-white scheme of things. Because her first relationship with a man was a failure she isn't about to put herself in a position where it could happen again. And so she's bored. Unnecessarily bored.

2. The Clean-Plate Club

Members-in-good-standing of the Clean-Plate Club are fond of telling you to "Finish what you start"... "Don't put off until tomorrow what you can do today"... "Keep your nose to the grindstone," and so on. The old-fashioned work ethic still keeps us bound to tasks we abhor just because we've been told it's cowardly or a sign of weakness to stop in midstream or to change course or to do something enjoyable. As children we change our minds all the time, but once we reach adulthood we're suddenly expected to know what we want, go for it and stick to it until age sixty-five. The middle-aged worker who wants to try something new risks the ridicule of his peers, the loss of his pension and the very real possibility that no one will want to hire someone who's changed careers at that age.

Karl was a skilled machinist in a large aircraft factory. He got on well with the other employees, arrived at work promptly and did his job. Everyone assumed he'd be there forever. Until the day he handed in his resignation to return to college and finish up his degree in psychology. Psychology! No one even knew Karl had been to college. Turned out he'd been biding his time until his children were grown. This was the step he needed to take to avoid life-stage boredom. His wife thought it was a great idea. She was tired of hearing about the assembly line, and ready for a change herself. Now that the kids were gone they could afford to cut back financially and live on their savings for a while.

Karl's friends and coworkers, though, were appalled. "What about your retirement?" they asked. "What if you can't find another job?" Karl was surprised by their strong resistance until his wife reminded him of his similar reaction when their son threatened to quit college in his senior year. We're all conditioned to resist change, suspect variety, fear the exceptions to the rule. But these are the very qualities that combat boredom best.

Learning to question whether something is really worth doing and whether it's worth doing now will eliminate a lot of deadwood from your life. Whether it's a book you're not enjoying, a task you don't want to complete or a job you hate, stop and ask yourself if there's really any reason to finish it. You'll be surprised at the number of boring activities you can simply abandon once you realize that you've

175

been mindlessly obeying the rigid messages your Crazy Me is sending you. Then you'll be free to do things, not because you *have* to, but because you *want* to.

3. *The Ghost of Emily Post*

Convention. How tightly it restricts the natural flow of things. Rather than responding afresh to each new situation in our lives we're programmed to see and judge ourselves and others through the tired, myopic eyes of the past—of how we're *supposed* to act. "It just isn't done" . . . "Going by the book" . . . "That's not kosher" . . . "Playing by the rules": words like these reduce our sense of ourselves as free beings. Even when we strike out to break new ground, we often find ourselves just reacting blindly to the prevailing norm rather than truly discovering a new way of looking at things. A lot of people who came of age in the 1960s have spent the better part of the '70s wondering what happened. How could all that hope and love, that energy and idealism, have turned to the cynicism and concern for creature comforts that mark the '70s? For every person whose life was profoundly changed by the peace movement, the women's movement, the civil-rights movement, or any other movement, there were at least ten others for whom "the revolution" itself was a convention. So it didn't take much, once the war in Vietnam was over and natural foods and macramé plant holders were no longer the preserve of the very young, to pick up the American Dream again—only this time "making it" was owning the local Earth Shoe franchise rather than moving up the ladder of General Motors.

Weddings, graduations, funerals, holidays—these intensely ritualized gatherings of the tribe are the best places to see how strong the force of convention can really be. On these occasions situational boredom reigns supreme. No one really wants to be there, but even the most iconoclastic among us is usually subdued by social expectations. You may not have worn a suit in years, but when Uncle Harry goes to the Great Beyond and your mother throws a fit because you planned to come to the funeral in your old madras plaid sports coat, I'm willing to bet you'll change your mind—and your jacket. It's not worth the trouble, we rationalize. And it may not be. Still, if we continue to give in, time after time, eventually we too forget that there are other ways to look at the world.

Phil is a frequent victim of stress-symptom boredom. He works in a high-powered law firm where twelve-hour days are the norm, and most of the time he loves it. But every few months it all starts to look the same—dull, meaningless, boring. A few days away, doing something unrelated to the law, is a sure-fire cure. But in Phil's office, this just isn't done. People are expected to put in the hours whether they're feeling productive or not. Phil is reluctant to challenge this convention. His Prosecuting Attorney tells him he's lazy, shiftless and irresponsible for even considering the possibility, while his Prophet of Doom warns that he can easily be replaced once the office finds out it can survive without him. So in spite of the fact that his Sane Me knows he'd do a better job if he could just let up once in a while, Phil trudges on, overworked and needlessly bored, all because he's afraid to buck a convention that makes no sense in terms of his own needs.

The ghost of Emily Post lurks everywhere. She's easier to see on the job and at social gatherings, but she's just as likely to intrude on your most intimate moments. Questions never asked, comments swallowed, suggestions censored—all because they might be rude—can smother even the most private times in a blanket of boredom.

4. Don't Talk to Strangers

"Safety first" . . . "Look before you leap" . . . "Don't go out on a limb" . . . "The boogie man will get you if you don't watch out. . . ." Fear can be a terrible taskmaster. Most of us learn very early on that the world is a dangerous place. Open any newspaper and you'll find stories about young girls raped, infants disappearing from campsites, boating accidents, random, senseless killings. Man seems, indeed, to be, as Thomas Hobbes said, "a wolf unto his fellow man." But these stories also contain a subliminal message, a message which, when multiplied by the millions of people who read them, is even more deadly. For we are being lured, day by day, into a state of passivity. Being careful has come to imply simply staying home, staying put: inertia. And in cutting our risks, we also cut our chances of having something surprising and wonderful happen.

Ever since she was a little girl, Marcia had been taught to be cautious. Especially with strangers. Her small family was close-knit and they trusted no one. When she spent summers with her grandparents at the beach she swam, built sandcastles, walked the shore—but always alone. They'd warned her against the other children. "They're too rough," they said. "They'll knock you down." And Marcia believed them.

Now she was back, but she wasn't a little girl anymore. She was a grown woman, here for a vacation. She knew now that she didn't have to spend all day either alone or in her grandparents' company. She wanted to make friends her own age. But every time she started to reach out, those early warnings echoed in her ears, and she withdrew. Fear-induced boredom had become a habit that was hard to break. We probably don't have anything in common anyway, she rationalized.

After several days of lying on the sand by herself, overhearing others' party plans, it occurred to her that this was a golden opportunity. She was a totally unknown quantity here. She could try making overtures to others without worrying about the consequences. After all, she'd be leaving again in a few weeks. But where to start? What to say?

Asking this question is the same thing as saying "I don't know how to please." Start where you are. In Marcia's case it was simply a matter of walking up to some relatively friendly-looking strangers and saying: "Hi. You know, I've been coming to this beach all my life, but I still don't know anybody. So I thought I'd come over and introduce myself." As it turned out, they'd been wondering about her for days, but were too shy themselves to make the first move. Before long Marcia was an accepted member of the local scene.

Now being cautious and withdrawn is sometimes the only practical way to get by. Sometimes the risks are greater than the potential rewards. There are better ways to make friends than by picking up hitchhikers on dark country roads, for instance. Not all strangers are approachable, nor is any place on earth as good as any other for expressing a point of view. At a banquet in Baghdad, obviously, it would be considered bad form to openly advocate a Jewish homeland. In most instances, however, playing it safe and keeping your mouth shut bears no correlation to saving your life, and there are times when valor is the better part of discretion.

179

5. Love Makes the World Go Around

All you need is love . . . according to the Beatles. Unfortunately, however, none of us ever gets as much as we think we need. Friends and a sense of community with our fellow beings have become essentials of modern life, but our search for love and, perhaps more importantly, the approval of others, can often turn into a wild-goose chase.

Well, maybe not "wild," for *believing and acting as if everyone must love and approve of you leads straight to boredom.* Because of our early conditioning, we've come to believe that if people knew what we were *really* like, we'd lose their love.

Many conceptions and misconceptions about the nature of love tend to crystallize during adolescence. This can be unfortunate. For adolescence is a time when our self-image is at an all-time low while our need for acceptance and the approval of others is at an all-time high. What do you remember about your teens? For most people it's a time of fads, conformity and confusion, of identities lost and found. We're so full of conflicting emotions in our teens that it often seems safer to take refuge in the crowd and wait until somehow we come out the other side of this darkness. In fact, what often happens is that our experiences as teenagers are so traumatic we never manage to get beyond them. At the first sign of rebellion we're shot down by both family and friends. When this happens on a regular basis it's easy to conclude that the price of individuality is love itself. It's then that we start subjecting our behavior to other people's vetoes instead of acting as our own judge.

Eric had a bad case of the "gotta-love-me's." When he first came to see me he was seething with frustration and had an ulcer to prove it. None of his friends could understand why Eric, of all people, should have an ulcer. "He's such a nice guy, so sweet and easygoing," they said. "Not at all the type to get an ulcer." Little did they know that the real Eric was not quite as agreeable as they thought. In fact, he was full of unexpressed opinions and dead-end desires. Because his life style had failed to reflect his true nature, however, he was not only angry, he was also bored.

From an early age Eric had loved music, theater and dance. His father, a physical-education instructor at the local community college, hadn't paid much attention at first to Eric's interest in ballet. His fledgling roles in school plays and talent shows indicated a real flair for dance, but at that point he was still young enough to be cute. As Eric entered his teens he found a dance teacher who took a genuine interest in his future, and he began to think seriously about a career in the theater. When his father realized that *his son* might actually turn out to be a dancer, he went into action. He ridiculed, he accused, he forbade Eric to participate in anything even remotely connected with the stage. For a while Eric fought back. His dance teacher offered to give him free lessons on the side. His close friends tried to convince him that he really had talent. On the other hand, there were a lot of rumors going around at school about "queers" and "fairies." Because of his lack of interest in more "macho" pursuits Eric was the number-one suspect. By the time Eric entered high school he had capitulated completely. He joined everything, he was everybody's pal, he even became a cheerleader and a model son. It was just about then that he started hitting the Rolaids!

Eric continued in this pattern as an adult. In large groups he always left decisions up to other people for fear of saying something controversial and unlikable. His favorite response was "Whatever." This made him easy to be with, but the price he paid for his ingratiating behavior was a bad

181

case of life-style boredom. Perhaps worst of all was his knowledge that none of his many friends really loved *him*. Rather, they seemed to like him for what he was not.

Gradually, Eric worked his way out of his bind. As he learned to respect himself and make his own desires clear, he made new friends who found his directness refreshing. He also began to see the folly of relying solely on the approval of others as a source of satisfaction. Better, he discovered, to rely on doing *what* you love—to pay less attention to others and more attention to yourself.

This not to say that any of us could or should want to withdraw from the social arena—it's far too rich a source of stimulation and pleasure for that. What I am suggesting is the existence of a middle ground. It's possible to carve out a space for yourself where you don't have to always be loved nor do you always have to get your own way. Standing up for yourself and accommodating others can coexist in peace once you have a clear sense of your own values, priorities and goals.

6. Don't Bite Off More Than You Can Chew

"You're working too hard" . . . "Don't overdo it" . . . "You've got too many irons in the fire" . . . If this advice sounds only too familiar, chances are you've got a good start on beating boredom. In my experience it's just when I'm at my most productive that I start hearing people tell me to put on the brakes. It's become a form of affection, a sign that you care, to caution those you love to "take care" of themselves. What we forget is that hard work and too much to do can be far more therapeutic than presiding over a life that's in perfect order but a dreadful bore.

Kate never answers the phone that she doesn't have to ask you to hang on a minute. Either her kids are scaling the refrigerator, she's cooking dinner for eight and something's burning, or she's in the darkroom and has a print in the developer. Kate's had twenty or thirty different jobs in her time—from waitressing in Paris to speechwriting in Washington, from social work in London to free-lance photography in L.A. Now she's decided to "settle down." But settling down for Kate is anything but routine. She's got a lot of friends, for one thing, all of whom vie for her time. She's writing a book, she reads voraciously, she's always behind. The house could stand a good cleaning, the children are on the wild side, the yard is a jungle. And Kate's never been happier. "Bored?" she asked me, incredulous. "How could I possibly be bored with all this going on? I get a little crazy sometimes, but I'm never bored."

Kate is a perfect example of the hidden rewards of overextending yourself. Now it's possible that she would be even more delighted with her life if it contained a little more order. But if you find yourself relying too heavily on budgets, schedules and lists of things to do, try relaxing the reins. Give up the illusion that you can control everything that happens to you. Let yourself be surprised by whatever the new day brings.

7. The Importance of Being Earnest

Why do so many people look back on their youth as the best years of their lives? Why does a baby have the power to charm even the gruffest adult? Perhaps it's because, as children, we haven't yet learned that "Life is grim, life is earnest, and the end is the grave." The sense of fun, the desire to play with others and the material universe is still very much with us. But it gets buried somehow under layers and layers of oughts and shoulds.

Fast Eddy is the best body and fender man on the West Coast. He's not only twice as fast as the average guy, but his work is always perfect the first time. No bumps, no waves, no complaints. Consequently he can work whenever he wants to. Body-shop owners vie for his time even though they know they can't hold him for long. For Eddy life is a laugh. I've never seen him seriously involved in anything but having fun and I've never seen him bored. Essentially, he's just a carefree kid of forty.

Eddy lives out of his van. Occasionally he crashes with his brother, house-sits for a friend or moves in with one of his several women admirers. When he's not working he buys a six-pack and goes to the beach, or maybe just plays with the kids on the block. Eddy has absolutely no ambition, no desire to make something of himself when he grows up. And in fact he'll probably never grow up since the cares and worries of adulthood don't hold any attraction for him. Eddy somehow never learned that life is a serious business and never accepted that other people's standards had anything to do with him. He once told me that when he was a young man he was sure he was going to die before he turned thirty. When he didn't, he just kept living as though the future didn't exist.

Most of us wouldn't want to join Eddy for very long. Hedonism, too, can lead to boredom after a while. But the next time you dent your fender, instead of devoting the next couple of days to estimates, police reports and insurance agents, try joining Eddy at the beach. A dented fender, or its equivalent, is not really so important either in the cosmic or the short-term sense. The humdrum traps we set for ourselves can only keep us back if we accept the notion that they are what's real and important about being alive.

8. Be Consistent

Hoist by your own petard. The bugaboo of consistency is one of boredom's best allies. And one of the hardest to shake. When you find yourself saying "I know what I like," be careful you're not just saying that you like what you knew yesterday. We don't always want or enjoy the same thing tomorrow that we liked today. But we're taught that to change our minds is a sign of weakness— when in fact it's directly related to our survival.

Where would we be if we couldn't learn from our mistakes, take up new positions, give up the old once it's been proven wrong? Back in the Dark Ages, that's where. Being open to experience means seeing yourself as a flexible being, a person who may feel one way one day, another way the next. In India the yogis have a saying—"A stiff body is an old body." That applies with equal force to boredom. A rigid person is a bored person.

Creativity involves looking at things from a different point of view—a point of view that's not necessarily consistent with how we saw things the day before, nor with how other people see them. Seeing things afresh, appreciating and courting novelty—this kind of flexibility is creativity. And creativity leaves no room for boredom.

I used to behave as though once I'd made plans or formed an opinion they were written in concrete. I'd been

185

taught to see myself as someone who carried through, who knew his own mind, who saw what he wanted and went for it—even if he'd stopped wanting it somewhere along the way. When I tried letting go of this idea for awhile I found to my surprise that, in fact, I'm a very moody, changeable person. The plans I make when I'm up make me uncomfortable when I'm down, and vice versa. The ideas, tastes and life style I'd committed myself to in my twenties no longer fit the person I'd become in my thirties.

My solution was simply to try to remain as flexible as possible. I've learned to expect my moods and plan my time accordingly. I have a friend who, if he wakes up feeling lousy, has little or no compunctions about cancelling his appointments for the day. Naturally this creates some problems, but it avoids lots of others. For one thing, no one has to put up with his snarls and whimpers. For another, his beastly moods are short-lived, since they don't have many complaints to feed on. I've tried to learn from his example by refusing, as much as possible, to be trapped into boredom by a rigid adherence to yesterday's plans.

Cultivating sensitivity to my own feelings has also opened my mind to experiences and people I would otherwise have rejected out of hand. Take something as simple as eating out. The other night I'd made plans to go to an Italian restaurant that had just opened. I'd been hungry for pasta that morning, but after a big lunch it no longer seemed appealing. So instead of going anyway, just because we had reservations, we decided to eat light. My friends suggested sushi, one of those dishes I'd been meaning to try but had never quite gotten around to because, let's face it, I didn't think I'd like raw fish. I still wouldn't call myself a convert, but the evening was far more stimulating than it would have been if we'd stuck to our guns, or changed our plans only to end up eating yet another cheeseburger!

9. The Walter Mitty Syndrome

"You've got your head in the clouds" . . . "Come down to earth" . . . "Keep your feet on the ground" . . . Admonitions against the pleasures of day-dreaming abound in the lexicon of the Crazy Me. Not only are such warnings unnecessary, but they cut us off from one of our greatest resources in the battle against boredom—the power of our own imagination.

Freddy was a dreamy kid. While the rest of us were off playing baseball, hanging out together at the drugstore, or leafing through each other's comics, Freddy would go off by himself for a few hours and then come back with a new idea. We all depended on him for inspiration when we ran out of things to do.

I lost track of Freddy during college. Then, a few years later, I ran into a mutual friend who told me that Freddy was president of his own Wall Street investment firm. Sounded as if Freddy was set for life in a comfortable and rather glamorous career. On my next trip to New York I called him but I was told that he'd sold the firm and moved to southern California. When I finally tracked him down he was running a garage that specialized in building and over-hauling race cars. "I thought you were a stockbroker. What happened?" I asked. "I was. But I got bored. Then I started thinking one winter day about what it would be like to live in California. I was interested in racing cars at the time, and in the middle of dreaming about the sun and the ocean and all those palm trees, it occurred to me that I could combine all my separate fantasies into one—and here I am." I realized then that Freddy had always had a strong need for stimulation. His intellectual boredom threshold was so low that nothing could hold his interest for long. Fortunately he also had a vivid imagination.

Freddy's seemingly endless capacity for self-renewal has to do with his ability to constantly come up with new and more interesting fantasy worlds to inhabit. Once he can visualize a new possibility for himself he starts to move in that direction and bam! he's no longer a stockbroker but a race-car mechanic. The key, of course, is learning to translate your inner life into some activity that will change your outer life. And for this it's essential to convince your Crazy Me to pay attention to the fertile creations of your imagination.

Say you see yourself as the hostess of a Washington salon, privy to all the inside gossip, one for whom the morning paper holds no surprises since you heard it all the night before. "Well, that's just impossible," scoffs your Crazy Me. "For one thing, you live in Kansas. And, for another, why would anyone in Washington want to meet you?" And that's the end of that fantasy. But it doesn't have to be. Now it's true that it's a long way from Kansas City to Washington, D.C., but there are elements you can salvage from this daydream. First, gathering together people you find interesting on a regular basis. And, second, the idea of you as the one who makes it all happen. Why not throw a party for all those people you think should meet but you haven't gotten around to introducing to each other yet? You may not turn out to be another Perle Mesta, but you can sure have one helluva barbeque!

10. Richard Cory

Whenever Richard Cory went down town,
  We people on the pavement looked at him:
He was a gentleman from sole to crown,
  Clean favored, and imperially slim.

And he was always quietly arrayed,
  And he was always human when he talked;
But still he fluttered pulses when he said,
  "Good-morning," and he glittered when he walked.

And he was rich—yes, richer than a king—
  And admirably schooled in every grace;
In fine, we thought that he was everything
  To make us wish that we were in his place.

So on we worked, and waited for the light,
  And went without the meat, and cursed the bread;
And Richard Cory, one calm summer night,
  Went home and put a bullet through his head.

The dream of perfection that Richard Cory's life embodied while it lasted lures all of us toward the shoals of boredom at one time or another. If we're constantly striving for an unattainable ideal—whether it's unlimited wealth, enduring fame, eternal physical beauty or instant spiritual enlightenment—we can hardly spend much time enjoying what we've got. So if you're always comparing yourself to others and coming up short—berating yourself for your less-than-perfect housekeeping, your less-than-infinite sexual endurance or whatever—chances are you're idealizing a fantasy, trying to make your life live up to an impossible dream. It's far better to spend your time setting up realistic standards for yourself based on what makes *you* feel comfortable than to try to satisfy your own internalized version of Richard Cory. What would happen if you, like Richard

Cory, did approach perfection? There'd be nowhere left to go—and boredom could not be far behind.

Closely allied with the idea that you've got to be perfect is the notion that you've got to be in complete and total control of your life. Obviously, this is another impossibility. There are just too many variables to contend with. Even coming close would require simplifying your existence to such an extent that it couldn't be anything but boring.

11. The Once and Future Life

"Things aren't what they used to be" . . . "Those were the good old days" . . . "You'll get your reward in heaven" . . . "Better save something for a rainy day" . . . People who are either stuck in the past or living for the future are invariably bored and dissatisfied with the present. We've all known folks for whom the Great Depression or World War II were peak experiences, the only time when they felt truly alive, and who continue to live as though time had stopped forty years ago. Then there are their counterparts on the other side of the coin—people who are waiting till the kids grow up to go to Europe, or spending all their energy making elaborate plans for a retirement they may never live to enjoy.

One of my colleagues, Todd, whose usual costume is a shirt with a button-down collar and a very narrow tie, told me that whenever he goes to a new barber he takes an old photograph with him, just to make sure the barber knows exactly what he wants. Todd hasn't had a new look since the fifties. He's closed himself off from any possibility that change might intrude and alter his carefully ordered universe. As a consequence, life is not only dull for Todd, but Todd himself is a bore. He's ruled by fear—fear of change, of novelty, of all the unpredictable surprises that could turn his extreme case of life-style boredom around.

Then there're Merle and Joe. All their lives they'd dreamed of having their own business, but the time was never right. Merle was busy bringing up the kids and Joe had a nine-to-five job he hated, but kept to pay the bills. They were afraid to borrow the money they would have needed to get going and more than a little scared of failing. They scrimped and saved but, just as they were on the verge of achieving their goal, Joe had a heart attack. He recovered but, what with all the medical expenses, their savings had disappeared along with their dream. All those years of fear-induced boredom, and all for nothing.

Living in the past or in the future may look like the easy way out when the present seems fraught with danger. In the long run, however, escaping from the here and now is a dead end that can only lead you straight from fear into boredom.

Not all of these dead giveaways apply equally well to everyone. Naturally our Crazy Me's all have their own particular patterns and ways of talking us into boredom. But there is a set of assumptions we hold in common. They have to do with inadequacy, and they form the heart of your Prosecuting Attorney's case against you. Just fill in the blanks—as many as you can think of—and, combined with the dead giveaways that really hit home, you'll have a good basis for recognizing the essential vocabulary of your own Crazy Me.

191

Personal Checklist of Crazy Me Statements

I'm too (fat, tall, old, etc.).

_____

_____

_____

_____

_____

I should (earn more money, love my mother, work harder, etc.).

_____

_____

_____

_____

_____

I'm not (good, smart, pretty, etc.) enough.

_____

_____

_____

_____

_____

Talking to Yourself

Now that you know what to listen for, here's how to talk back. As an effective weapon against boredom, talking to yourself is the next best thing to decisive action—and generally precedes it. For in order to move out of boredom, negative feelings and beliefs must not only be identified, but contradicted and beaten into the ground.

Essentially, what makes the Crazy Me crazy is its inability to distinguish fact from fiction. The Crazy Me has no compunctions about saying things that are either absolutely false or that, at best, are only partially true.

Let's assume that you've been asked to go water-skiing for the first time (something you've always said you wanted to try) but you haven't decided whether or not to accept. You're feeling rather uncomfortable about the decision. That, in itself, is a clue. When you're having negative feelings it's usually a sign that the Crazy Me is putting in an appearance. Now is the time to ask yourself to be very specific about what you're feeling and believing about water-skiing. Maybe you feel scared. ("If I go I'm sure to get hurt." "I'll probably drown.") Maybe you feel inadequate. ("I'm no good at sports." "I look terrible in a bathing suit." "I'll make a fool of myself."). Or even guilty. ("I've got too much work to do." "I should be spending time with my family.") *But believing and feeling something doesn't make it true.*

Let's take the first two statements. Once you know that your Prophet of Doom is forecasting certain injury or even probable death you can contradict this belief. Clearly, if you go water-skiing, it is neither certain that you will get hurt nor probable that you will drown. The possibility of injury or death is always with us, of course, but it is exactly that—a statistically unlikely possibility. Knowing that your Crazy Me is wrong, you can tell it: "These assumptions that you're making are false and I refuse to act on them." "Well," responds a chastened Prophet of Doom, "you *might* get hurt." "Now that," you can triumphantly respond, "is quite another matter. It's true that I may get hurt. But it's far more likely that I won't. And I'm willing to take the risk in order to do something I've always wanted to try."

If you find you're feeling inadequate or guilty, it's safe to

193

assume that your Prosecuting Attorney is in charge. Let's examine those allegations more carefully. So you're not Billie Jean King or Bruce Jenner. The sporting life has never been your bag. So what? So you're not Marilyn Monroe or Tarzan and your bathing suit's a little baggy here or a little too snug there. So what? So you fall off your water skis or, worse yet, never get on them. So what? Acting on these feelings, even if they have some basis in reality, is pretty likely to be more boring than going water-skiing in spite of them. In these cases, the best response would go something like this: "What you're saying may be true and it may not, but I'm not willing to spend another weekend at home with nothing to do just because my bathing suit doesn't fit. That's just not a very good reason to refuse."

Feelings of guilt need to be examined from another, more positive, point of view. Water-skiing instead of working or spending time with your family may very well contribute to your effectiveness on the job or as a parent. But we're so conditioned to look at our actions with a critical eye that this way of perceiving what we do may escape us altogether—or else be dismissed as just another rationalization. Given the two ways of looking at this decision—"I shouldn't go water-skiing because I should be doing something else" or "Going water-skiing will give me just the boost I need to get on with the rest of my life"—you have to decide just how much weight to give your other responsibilities. Can they be performed at some other time? Are they really important? Do you really have to do them at all? Nine times out of ten, answering such questions honestly will lead you to the inescapable conclusion that the more positive way of looking at your motives is correct. The things you think you "ought to" do are just not that essential. Besides, they're generally dull and boring. The things you want to do are, in the long run, far more important and

194

lots more fun. So your response to your Prosecuting Attorney might be: "No, I can do that work some other time. I deserve a day off. I do want to spend more time with the children, but before I do that I need some time for myself. I'm a better parent when I'm with them because I want to be there."

As you begin to develop new habits and methods for refuting the Crazy Me, remember that, in most cases, you've had twenty years or more to practice thinking crazy. Learning how to think sane takes time. When you fail, the sane way to look at it is to say that it's no big disaster, and next time you'll do better. Also, try to avoid the trap of dwelling on *why* your Crazy Me operates in one particular way or another. This can be a fun, intellectual game, but it won't change the present one iota. And you might well be wasting time that could be much more profitably spent.

Dialogues

Talking to yourself—your real self—takes practice, for the Prosecuting Attorney and the Prophet of Doom are both masters of disguise. The dialogues that follow are but a small sampling of their various masks. In these dialogues the Crazy Me, in one of his or her many personas, is talking to the Sane Me. In the first version the Sane Me is gradually overcome by the Crazy Me, while in the second version the Sane Me effectively silences the Crazy Me. After the first dialogue there is an analysis of what the Crazy Me is doing and how, in each case, you can draw on the Sane Me's resources. Chances are you'll be able to construct some comparable dialogues of your own since, like fingerprints, no two Crazy Me's are ever exactly alike.

195

Monday-Morning Malcolm

Scene: It's Monday morning. You had a family reunion yesterday and ran out of hamburgers and beer before half the people had eaten.

Malcolm: Great performance at the supermarket yesterday. I can't believe you ran out of both hamburgers *and* beer. How the hell did that happen?

Sane Me: Well, uh, I guess I didn't plan things very well. Then Uncle Harry brought the twins and Fred went off his diet.

Malcolm: You could have bought extra food like I've told you before. If you had too much you could always freeze it. And beer never goes bad.

Sane Me: Well, I didn't have that much money with me and I forgot my checkbook.

Malcolm: You could have gone to Rebozo's and charged it.

Sane Me: Oh, I forgot about that. Come to think of it, I didn't have my credit card either, and my car was almost out of gas. . . .

Malcolm, the Prosecuting Attorney, has perfect hindsight. He always knows exactly what you should have done and doesn't hesitate to point it out to you. If you listen to Malcolm you'll end up feeling so demoralized that you'll either never give another barbeque or you'll be so uptight about the possibility of something going wrong that you won't enjoy it. Either way you'll be adding to your potential boredom. The way to deal with Malcolm is to admit your past mistakes, and then go on to discuss the future. Put yesterday behind you where it belongs by steadfastly refusing to beat yourself up for a past error.

The Sane Me Talks Back

Malcolm: Great performance at the supermarket yesterday. I can't believe you ran out of both hamburgers *and* beer. How the hell did that happen?

Sane Me: I didn't plan correctly. Made the mistake of not buying enough food.

Malcolm: Jesus, half the people there had to eat hot dogs and drink Pepsi.

Sane Me: I don't really want to talk about yesterday. There's nothing I can do now to change what happened. How about helping me plan the next barbecue?

Malcolm: Do you know how embarrassed I was by that scene?

Sane Me: Yes I do. But making me feel bad about myself isn't going to put more hamburgers on yesterday's table, so let's move on to next weekend's party.

Malcolm: Well, I just can't put it out of my mind.

Sane Me: You'll just have to because we've got too much planning to do to indulge you now.

197

Up From Boredom, Down From Fear

Polly the Perfectionist

Scene: Your best friend told you a secret, made you promise not to tell, and you inadvertently let the cat out of the bag.

Polly: Do you remember when Sally told you Betty's pregnant? And she asked you not to say anything to Betty?

Sane Me: Yeah, but let me explain.

Polly: How could you be so stupid? You not only told her you knew about it, but you were actually congratulating her before she even got her coat off.

Sane Me: Well, I was happy for her and it just sort of spurted out.

Polly: How could you be so dumb? Don't you know what this can do to your friendship with Sally? She'll probably never speak to you again, let alone trust you. And I wouldn't blame her, would you?

Sane Me: Well, uh . . . uh . . .

Polly is perfect. She never makes mistakes. She tries to get you to mend your ways by invoking fear and guilt. If she succeeds, you'll end up paralyzed by fear of failure and its inevitable consequence, boredom. Polly's big mistake is in thinking you are capable of being as perfect as she is, that all you need is the proper motivation. She is, of course, wrong. And you can tell her so by simply refusing to live by her impossible standards.

198

The Sane Me Talks Back

Polly: Do you remember when Sally told you Betty's pregnant? And she asked you not to say anything to Betty?

Sane Me: Yeah. Boy, did I blow it.

Polly: How could you be so stupid?

Sane Me: I made a mistake all right. But there is no sense crying over spilled milk. All I can do is admit it and go on from here.

Simon Legree

Scene: It's Saturday morning. You're barely awake. You've been looking forward to reading the paper over several cups of coffee and then spending the day lazing around the house watching a little football, talking to your friends, puttering. You start to pour your second cup of coffee. . . .

Simon: Hey, What are you doing?

Sane Me: Pouring myself another cup of coffee.

Simon: You're awake. What do you need that for? We've got a long day ahead of us. The leaves have to be cleaned out of the gutters. The long-range forecast says snow is on the way, and you know what a bitch it is to get the leaves out if it snows and then freezes. Hell, you'll be putting new gutters up in the spring if you don't do it now. Get up. Get your boots on. Get the ladder out of the garage.

199

Sane Me: Well, I kinda planned on getting some rest. I've been working real hard and I need some time off.

Simon: Ah, come on. Cleaning the leaves out will be relaxing. After all, it's not like the work you do in the office all week. You'll like it once you get started.

Sane Me: (weakening) Well, let me have another cup of coffee and I'll get to it.

Simon: What a procrastinator you are. It's already ten o'clock. Let's get the gutters done by, say, one or two o'clock, and then after lunch you can start on the window ledges. They're all chipped and peeling. If you don't get them painted in the next week or two they'll really start to deteriorate. You wouldn't want to have to replace them all, would you? You know how expensive that would be.

Sane Me: Well . . . uh . . . uh. . . Just let me have half a cup and I'll get right on it.

Simon: I'll tell you what. Why don't you just put it in one of those plastic cups and bring it outside with you?

Sane Me: Okay, let's go.

If Simon had his way you'd work twenty-five hours a day. He values only one thing—getting things done. Keeping your nose to the grindstone with no time off for good behavior. And he'll resort to just about anything to prevent you from taking a break. If you allow Simon's tyranny to continue you'll never be free of boredom. Talking back to Simon requires standing firm.

The Sane Me Talks Back

Simon: Hey, what are you doing?

Sane Me: Pouring myself another cup of coffee.

Simon: You're awake. What do you need that for? We've got a long day ahead of us . . . etc . . . .etc.

Sane Me: No, old buddy. Today is my day off. I'm gonna sit around, drink coffee and beer, eat a big lunch and watch a few football games. This is *my* day.

Simon: Are you kidding? What about the leaves in the gutters? Do you know how hard it will be to get them out later? Do you know how much new ones cost?

Sane Me: It'll be a bitch to get them out. And new ones cost more than I can afford. But I need a day off. I've been working too hard. If just bumming around for a while ends up costing me more money or creating more work, then that's the way it is. I'll take my chances. But there's no way I'm going to work today.

Simon: Okay, let's make a deal. How about if we work till noon and then knock off?

Sane Me: Nope, I've made up my mind. Today is my day off and I'm not going to do a thing.

The Good Samaritan

Scene: You're caught in a traffic jam, you're thirty minutes late for a dinner party, and

201

you've just remembered it's your mother's birthday, when the man in front of you bangs into a Cadillac.

Good
Samaritan: You'd better pull over. You were a witness, after all.

Sane Me: I don't have time. Sorry.

Good
Samaritan: What kind of person are you, anyway? You forgot your mother's birthday, you're late again, and now you won't even stop to help someone in need.

Sane Me: You're probably right. You know, if I stopped now I could run to a telephone and call my mom. And then I could call and apologize for being late. That way I could make everybody happy. . . .

If the Good Samaritan has his way you'll not only be your brother's keeper but the rest of the world's as well. It's all your responsibility. Relieving yourself of the Good Samaritan means sharing the burden a bit, knowing that you can trust others to help too and realizing that acting "irresponsibly" once in a while is not the beginning of the end. Otherwise you'll be so busy making sure the rest of the world's okay, or so immersed in guilt because you couldn't save them all, that you'll be unable to pay attention to your own needs for stimulation.

The Sane Me Talks Back

Good
Samaritan: You'd better pull over. You were a witness, after all.

Talking To Your "Self"

Sane Me: I don't have time. Sorry.

Good Samaritan: What kind of person are you, anyway? You forgot your mother's birthday, you're late again, and now you won't even stop to help someone in need.

Sane Me: You're right. Under other circumstances I would stop. But tonight it's someone else's turn to save the world.

Good Samaritan: What about your mother and all those people you've kept waiting? Aren't you going to call them and apologize?

Sane Me: My mother knows that I love her. As for the dinner party, calling won't get me there any faster. You may think I've been irresponsible, but I'm doing the best I can.

Eartha Inertia

Scene: You are sitting around after dinner on a Thursday night thinking about what you can do before going to bed.

Sane Me: You know, it might be interesting to watch that program on underwater mammals.

Eartha: Nah. Whales and dolphins again. I've seen that routine ten times already this year.

Sane Me: How about taking a walk down to the newsstand. They just added a whole new section. Maybe there'll be something interesting there.

203

Eartha: Nah! Probably just a lot of girlie magazines.

Sane Me: Well, how about taking a ride over to that new ice-cream parlor for a soda?

Eartha: Nah! I'm getting too fat.

Sane Me: Well, how about calling Claire and seeing if she'd like to bowl a couple of games?

Eartha: She's probably busy, and besides, I think Thursday night is league night and we probably wouldn't get an alley before 11:30.

Eartha Inertia can go on all night unless you find a way to break her veto power. She can always find a way to say no, to keep you stuck in boredom, but when called upon to suggest more interesting alternatives she draws a blank. The boredom solution is to make a decision. It hardly matters what you decide to do. The important thing is to stick by it and *do something.*

The Sane Me Talks Back

Sane Me: You know, it might be interesting to watch that program on underwater mammals.

Eartha: Nah! Whales and dolphins again. I've seen that routine ten times already this year.

Sane Me: Yeah, I have too. But this program might have something new to say.

Eartha: Probably not.

Sane Me: Do you have anything better to suggest?

204

Talking To Your "Self"

Eartha: Nah! Nothing sounds very good to me.

Sane Me: Okay. Then we'll try the TV program and if that doesn't work out we'll discuss some other possibilities.

Molly the Mindreader

Scene: You are thinking about inviting a new and fascinating coworker out for a drink.

Sane Me: I'm gonna do it. I'm gonna take a chance. I'll call him up and see if he'd like to go out for a drink. Just off the top of my head. Spur of the moment. You only go around once.

Molly: I wouldn't do that. He'll probably think you're too aggressive. I can tell he doesn't go for that.

Sane Me: Why would he think I'm too aggressive? He might think I just wanted to spend time with him.

Molly: I noticed the other day when the ERA petition went around that he didn't sign it. I can tell he's not your type. Besides, if you ask him out, he'll lose respect for you.

Sane Me: Well, maybe I can strike up a conversation with him just before it's time to leave. Then it would seem more spontaneous.

Molly: I wouldn't do that. He closed his door to take a call in the office today. I'm sure it was his girlfriend. He looks like the type that's been going with someone since high school. I can tell.

205

Molly has all sorts of fantasies about why people do the things they do and what they are really feeling and thinking. The trouble is Molly's fantasies have little to do with reality except insofar as they keep you from reaching out and getting involved. The best comeback for Molly is to put her fantasies to the test by finding out what's really going on.

The Sane Me Talks Back

Sane Me: I'm gonna do it. I'm gonna take a chance. I'll call him up and see if he'd like to go out for a drink. Just off the top of my head. Spur of the moment. You only go around once.

Molly: I wouldn't do that. He'll probably think you're too aggressive. I can tell he doesn't go for that.

Sane Me: Why would he think I'm too aggressive? He might think I just wanted to spend time with him.

Molly: I noticed the other day when the ERA petition went around that he didn't sign it. I can tell he's not your type. Besides, if you ask him out, he'll lose respect for you.

Sane Me: He might lose respect for me, but if he does, that's life. I might as well find out how he feels about the things I believe in before I get too involved. If he doesn't like aggressive women the best time to find out is right now. No sense in deceiving him into thinking I'm something I'm not.

206

Molly: Well, why don't you wait and check out his feelings before you leap into something? He probably already has a girlfriend anyway.

Sane Me: I won't wait because I'd like to go out tonight. And as for his imaginary girlfriends, there's only one way to find out if they're real. And that's to take a chance and ask him out.

Powerless Pete

Scene: You and Pete have just learned that one of your superiors has put in for early retirement.

Sane Me: Wow! What a surprise. Fogle retiring at fifty-five. I thought he'd be here until he was ninety. I wonder if I've got a chance at his job.

Pete: You might just get lucky, but I doubt it.

Sane Me: I wonder if there's something I could do to make it known that I'd like to be considered.

Pete: There's not much you can do in these situations. Best to just wait it out and see what happens.

Sane Me: Maybe I could go to Ms. Fenson and ask her to keep me in mind.

Pete: Naw. Best to be quiet. If it's meant to be it's meant to be. If not, there's nothing you can do about it. Qué sera, sera. . . .

If you listen to Powerless Pete you will quickly get the

impression that there is very little you can do about anything. No sense in trying to determine your own destiny since you are obviously at the mercy of fate. This attitude is guaranteed to keep you in a static position—the bored victim of your own inaction. Pete can only reign, however, if you sit back and accept his assessment of the situation.

The Sane Me Talks Back

Sane Me: Wow! What a surprise. Fogle retiring at fifty-five. I thought he'd be here until he was ninety. I wonder if I've got a chance at his job.

Pete: You might just get lucky, but I doubt it.

Sane Me: There's more than luck involved. I'll go talk to Ms. Fenson and let her know that I'm interested in the job.

Pete: That won't do any good. They've probably already made up their minds. There's nothing you can do.

Sane Me: Maybe if I demonstrate a little more initiative they'll sit up and take notice.

Pete: Aw, stop dreaming. There's nothing to be done. Qué sera, sera.

Sane Me: This may not work but I'm gonna give it my best shot. I've got nothing to lose, and even if I fail at least I'll know I tried.

Once you can identify the voices of the Crazy Me, and know how to talk back, you have the basic tools you need to banish boredom—at least temporarily. But kicking the habit for good requires more than a working knowledge of one's conditioning.

Coming up from boredom and down from fear involves mastering five basic steps: First, focusing on yourself— asking what am I feeling, what am I believing, thinking or saying to myself, and what am I doing? Second, recognizing when your feelings, thoughts and actions are reflecting the Crazy Me. Third, contradicting the Crazy Me with sane self-statements. Fourth, making a decision. And fifth, acting on it. So far we've covered the first three steps pretty thoroughly. You're aware of your own boredom and you know how to contradict it. But to translate that awareness into action, to get off the fence after perhaps a lifetime of inertia, can only be accomplished through meticulous changes in your actual behavior.

3
Gambits

7
Reconnaissance and Battle Plans

Nothing eliminates boredom more successfully than engaging in the search for ways to end it.

—Bruno Bettelheim, Dialogue with Mothers

Here's where we get down to brass tacks. You know what boredom is, you understand its causes, and you've learned to talk back to your Prosecuting Attorney and Prophet of Doom. So where do you go from here?

As a general rule, you can't take effective action until you've made an accurate assessment of the problem. Once you know exactly where you are now, you can decide where you want to go. An awareness of the unique dimensions and characteristics of your boredom problem will clarify whether major or minor changes are called for in your life.

Say you're bored with your marriage. Essentially you have three choices: you can leave; you can stay in the situation and try to find alternative ways of getting stimulation; or you can accept things the way they are. Your decision will depend on your evaluation of the situation as a whole.

The exercises that follow will aid you in making this all-important evaluation in many different areas of your life. You may find, after completing them, that your marriage doesn't look so bad after all. There may be some rocky patches here and there—boredom in the bedroom, a lack of intellectual stimulation, or just a general sense of over-familiarity—but if your relationship is only sporadically boring, you'll probably want to stay and work on those specific problems from within. Or you may decide to stay and look for alternative sources of outside stimulation in those particular areas—an occasional fling to spice things up, new friends with fresh ideas, and so forth. If you can't find even a glimmer of fun, excitement, or common ground, then it's probably time to hit the road. But what if you're still in love, you've tried to find stimulating alternatives to the boring areas in your relationship without much success and you don't know what to do next? It may be time to bite the bullet—to accept those aspects of your mate and your relationship that are not as scintillating as you'd like, and just refuse to let them obscure the good things you have together. Compromise is not necessarily a bad thing if your relationship is, on the whole, a good one.

In this chapter we're going to get very specific. First you'll have a chance to tune in to your own very personal patterns of boredom—from what bores you to where, when and with whom you're bored. Then we'll explore some of the resources you've already got for finding a way out of the vicious circle created by boredom and fear. And finally we'll work on creating a tailor-made plan that will gradually change the hidebound system of thoughts, actions and feelings that have kept you bored into a dynamic force for change.

I've come up with four different but interlocking ways of exploring your boredom: the Boredom Inventory, the Boredom Diary, the Habit Inventory and the Feeling Inventory. Take the time to complete each exercise *in writing*.

Writing down your responses is absolutely essential.

You can't arrive at an accurate picture of the problem unless your thinking is rigorously clear. And writing forces this kind of mental clarity just as going to a therapist and talking forces you to clarify your thoughts in order to communicate them to someone else in a way they can understand.

You may want to treat yourself to a personal boredom book. Buy a small notebook at the five-and-dime to carry around with you. This will be especially handy in keeping the Boredom Diary and the Feeling Inventory. You can also use it to note down new thoughts and ideas for coping with your boredom.

If the prospect of doing all these exercises at once is a little overwhelming, remember what you've learned about the importance of finding your own rhythms. Do one, give yourself a rest and then, when you're ready and eager once more, do another one. When you've finished, take the time to think about how each exercise relates to the other three.

The Boredom Inventory

The Boredom Inventory is simply a checklist of the areas in all our lives that most often fall prey to boredom. It's essential to examine these areas periodically—the equivalent of an annual physical—to make sure they haven't succumbed to boredom while you weren't looking!

You may wish to use this Inventory as a skeleton on which to base your own more personal and detailed inventory, adding categories that apply specifically to you. You might want to break down certain categories into their component parts—the various aspects of your household tasks or the different activities that make up your job, for instance. You can also add the actual sports and hobbies you engage in most, and list the names of your friends and relatives. Then you'll have a personalized Boredom Inventory for future reference. If you make a note of the date each time you use the inventory, briefly recording any action taken, it can also serve as a kind of continuing boredom report card over the years.

	Date: Action	Date: Action	Date: Action
Work			
Income- producing			
Household tasks			
Child care			
Other			
Relationships			
Husband/wife/ lover/ housemates			
Children			
Friends			
In-laws			
Brothers and sisters			
Boss			
Employees			
Social or business acquaintances			
Strangers			

	Date: Action	Date: Action	Date: Action
Sex			
Social Activities			
Political work			
Civic involvement			
Parties			
Guests			
Church			
Clubs			
Sports			
Hobbies			
Life styles			
Eating habits			
Clothing and cosmetics			
Shelter			
Furniture, interior decor			
Household routines			
Money and your relationship to it			
Saving			
Spending			
Credit			
Investments			

	Date: Action	Date: Action	Date: Action
Addictions			
TV			
Alcohol			
Drugs			
Cigarettes			
Eating			
Sleeping			
Travel			
For work			
For pleasure			

Boredom Diary

The next step in pinpointing your personal patterns of boredom is keeping a detailed Boredom Diary. It will provide you with an invaluable record of exactly when, where and with whom boredom occurs.

Starting now, keep a record of your activities for seven days. (A sample page follows.) Whenever you change major activities (eating, shopping, working, driving and so on) note down what you've been doing, how long you've been doing it, where you are and whom you're with. Also try thinking about what kind of boredom you've been experiencing. Is it momentary boredom (calling the airport only to hear the same recorded message fifty times before you get through), watching the drier roll at the laundromat because you forgot your book), life-style boredom (a job you can't stand, or constant rather than sporadic apathy and inertia), relationship boredom (a sagging love affair, a friend who keeps you on the phone for hours) or what?

What was your Prosecuting Attorney and/or Prophet of Doom telling you that kept you bored?

In filling out my own Boredom Diary I found that there were certain times of the day when I was most likely to be bored, some activities that always bored me and others that were only boring if I did them too often, stuck with them too long or was in a lousy mood to begin with. Some people, although they aren't boring in themselves, seemed to land in the doldrums with me more often than others. These are the kinds of patterns to watch for when you analyze your own results. It's also helpful to think about where your stimulation is coming from when you're not bored—are you playing the juicer, egghead, player or goalie?

Date:
Day:

Activity	Location	With Whom	Kind of Boredom	Prosecuting Attorney STATEMENT	Prophet of Doom STATEMENT	Source of Stimulation

8 A.M. 7 A.M. 6 A.M.

Habit Inventory

Using the activities you've listed in the Boredom Diary, you can start to create a Habit Inventory. Look carefully for the activities that recur more or less regularly throughout the days and list them on the daily and weekly charts that follow—such things as when you do the laundry, pay the bills, go out to dinner, call your mother, and so forth. At this point try not to judge whether these habits are good or bad, boring or interesting. Also be on the lookout for the things you do that are so routine that you've neglected to even write them down in the Diary. This information will come in very handy when we start to deal with concrete ways to change your actual behavior.

Daily Habits

Morning:

Noon:

Afternoon:

Dinner:

Weekly Habits

Monday:

Tuesday:

Wednesday:

Thursday:

Friday:

Reconnaissance and Battle Plans

Saturday:

Evening:

Sunday:

Feeling Inventory

Creating a Feeling Inventory involves keeping track of your physical, mental and emotional ups and downs for a month or so. At the end of the day, take some private time for yourself and make some notes on your activities and how they affected you. A sample entry might go something like this:

3:00 pm
Tennis date with Bob. Before the match I was physically sluggish (had a late lunch) and a little depressed—probably thinking about Suzy again. I played well, though, felt agile and alert, like I was really in control of my game, and afterwards, when I got home, I was more relaxed than I've been all week.

5:00 pm
Dad called with a long story about Uncle Sam. Felt bored and guilty for not paying better attention. Prosecuting Attorney at work, no doubt.

5:30–7:30 pm
Watched the news. Same stories over and over but couldn't seem to get up the energy to turn it off. Probably inertial boredom.

7:45 pm
D. called to see if I'd eaten yet. Decided to go

221

out for a hamburger together. Cheered me up right away.

And so forth.

This kind of journal is a good way of tracing the complex interplay between what happens to you, what you do and how you feel. At the end of the month, read it over, looking carefully at what makes you feel good, bad or indifferent. Also see if you can spot the entrances and exits of the Prosecuting Attorney and the Prophet of Doom. Now you're in a position to identify the times and circumstances when you almost always feel lousy: I'm never comfortable driving to work. I'm usually irritated when I'm spending time with the children. Gardening always leaves me feeling depressed, or whatever—and the times when you feel good: I'm always at my best when I'm entertaining friends. I love to read in bed. Working with my hands is invigorating, and so on. This information about yourself is a way of tracing boredom through some of the other negative feelings that are its frequent companions. The positive feelings are leads to behavior that's just about guaranteed to pull you up from boredom and down from fear.

It's a good idea to discuss what you're doing with your partner or roommate. Tell them that if this is going to work your notebook has to remain private, and ask them to promise not to read it. You can also write on the front: PRIVATE. DO NOT READ IF FOUND. These security measures may not always work, of course, so try not to tempt the fates too much. Think of ways to insure your privacy—like keeping it in your purse or pocket most of the time.

The next exercise has to do with exploring the resources already present in your memory and in your imagination that can provide you with clues to the best boredom solutions for you.

The Fantasy-Reality Discrepancy Technique

Sit back, relax and sift through your life history for all the "might-have-beens," the "what-ifs"—the men or women you might have married, the places you could have gone, the careers you almost pursued. What opportunities did you pass by? Which dreams have you abandoned? What would your life be like if? . . . Stick fairly close to reality here. Things that actually *could* have happened if you'd let them.

As you remember each one, note it down. Just let them flow without dwelling on any one for long. If you do a thorough job, you'll end up with a fantastic number of leads to hidden or forgotten dreams, urges, talents and desires that you have yet to fully explore.

The interests and choices of earlier days can give us useful information on aspects of ourselves that may have gotten tucked away over the years. But just because you wanted to be the first person to land on the moon when you were twelve doesn't mean that's still going to be number one on your priority list!

To get in touch with how your present-day fantasies can help overcome boredom, take a look at the areas you've already identified as boring on the Boredom Inventory and use your imagination to construct some scenarios of how you would like it to be. Be sure to write them down and include as much as you can—from the mundane to the profane—in as much detail as possible. Here, be just as extravagant as you like.

Now you can compare your past and present dreams, hopes and fantasies with the reality of the here and now. Start looking for some of the areas where the twain might meet, where fantasy and reality are not really so very far apart. If the discrepancies seem too great, think of ways you can translate the substance of the fantasy into a form that would change the present content of your life. For instance, winning the Indianapolis 500 might convert to exploring the various opportunities for auto racing in your own particular neck of the woods. The Nobel Peace Prize might translate into some local political activity—reconciling pro- and anti-busing factions, for example.

With the information you've just collected and the principles, conceptual techniques and examples presented earlier in the book you're now in a position to do something about your own boredom.

The first step is to pick out the various areas in your life where you have a boredom problem. Look over the first four exercises and list all the clues. The Boredom Inventory will help you pinpoint *what* bores you and the Boredom Diary will give you ideas on when, where and with whom you're most often bored. With the Habit Inventory you can look at which routines reinforce your boredom and which ones work against it. The Feeling Inventory can assist you in identifying those physical, mental and emotional states that may not feel like boredom but are, in fact, manifestations or symptoms of its presence. Fatigue, for example. When you're feeling tired and you write it down, the very act of making your feeling explicit can help you see that it's really boredom you're experiencing—especially if you just got up after a good night's sleep! You'll also begin to see the patterns that lead to boredom in various feelings that formerly seemed completely random and mysterious.

A short sample list might look something like this:

> What bores me:
> Child care
> Household tasks, especially dusting and
>   vacuuming
> In-laws
> Hobbies
> TV

Reconnaissance and Battle Plans

When, where, and with whom:
Lunch
After dinner
Sundays
At home
At the market
With spouse in social situations

Habits that lead to boredom:
Watching TV in evenings
Lunching with the same people every day

I feel uncomfortable:
Alone at night
Cooking
Trying to concentrate for long periods of time

Now, rather than trying to tackle everything at once, choose one area to work on, then make a plan of attack based on clear and simple behavioral goals. Any plan, in order to succeed, must be (1) explicit, (2) realistic, and (3) end with a definable action or goal to be achieved.

Let's say the problem you choose to work on is your lack of interesting hobbies. Your first task is to think of something you'd like to do. Here's where the last exercise can really help. Looking down your list of "might-have-beens" you see that you once considered majoring in music but changed your mind because it wasn't practical. You also notice that in one of your favorite fantasies you're being showered with roses after your singing debut at La Scala. Your Feeling Inventory confirms that you always feel good when you're doing something related to music. Checking your Habit Inventory you see that there's nothing you do regularly, like practicing the piano, singing in a choir or even warbling in the shower that takes advantage of this way out of boredom. So you choose a goal.

Singing at La Scala is one possible choice but, at this

point in your vocal career, not a very realistic one. So you scale down your goal to something you can accomplish in the near future—beginning singing lessons, for instance. And you make an explicit, step-by-step plan.

In this instance you might start by checking out the vocal coaches in your area, finding out about their reputations and areas of expertise and talking to the most likely prospects. Then you have only to choose a teacher and set up a schedule of lessons and practice periods that would fill those spots in your day when you're most likely to be bored.

This all sounds like eminently sensible advice, right? It would be surprising, however, if you didn't run into a lot of resistance from your Crazy Me—especially at first. And here's where the conceptual techniques you've already learned come into play. It's important to include, as an integral part of your plan, a space to examine your thoughts, feelings and actions (or inaction) for clues to the source of any resistance you may be feeling. Then you'll have the information you need to talk yourself up from boredom and back to sanity.

Space for reevaluation is also essential. You're a changing person and, as you begin to implement various plans for coping with boredom, you'll find that solutions that worked well at first may need rethinking. As you become more confident you'll start to take risks, so your early plans may begin to seem a little tame.

This approach to behavioral change works whether your boredom problem is short-term or long-term, mild or severe. When working on problems that may call for major shifts in priorities or life style, however, it's particularly important not to lose sight of the central core of who you are. You're not out to change *yourself*. Rather, your task is to free the Sane Me from the constraints, fears and inhibi-

226

tions that imprison you in boredom. Behaviorally, this requires that you change the things you do in order to make it easier for the Sane Me to take charge and remain in control. This is very different from trying to change who you are.

Another key to success when it comes to long-term changes is remembering that it's probably not going to happen overnight. If you apply the planning process I've described I can assure you that change will occur—that what you end up with will be very different from what you started with. But it's also likely that what you end up with will surprise you.

Let's look at the case of Marion and Jeff. Jeff was bored with sex—not just sex with Marion, but sex period. He'd had a few extramarital affairs but they didn't seem to hold his interest for long. When Jeff came to see me we set up a behavioral plan of action together. His goal was to have one interesting sexual encounter per week. He made a list of people he'd been curious about sexually, and another list of places to go that he found erotic—the beach, the art museum, a jazz club he liked and so forth. Each week he invited someone on List A to go somewhere on List B. Jeff expected a variety of responses—rejection, wild rolls in the hay, suspicion and so on. But what he got came as a complete surprise. It was friendship.

Jeff had never thought of himself as lonely. After all, he and Marion had a whole set of people they saw socially. But what he discovered was that there were very few people he knew on his own—people who knew him and liked him because they had something special in common. What Jeff had mistaken for sexual attraction was, instead, the recognition of mutual interests that might include sex but weren't limited to it.

Once Jeff realized that what he really wanted and needed

were richer, more satisfying friendships, he changed his goals accordingly. He began cultivating interesting men as well as women and going places he'd never been before. As his social life became more stimulating, his sex life with Marion improved dramatically, for he no longer expected it to carry the burden of satisfying all his other needs for stimulation as well.

By using the five techniques I've devised for identifying and finding your own ways out of boredom, by creating plans based on explicit steps to realistic goals, and by continually talking back to your Crazy Me, you'll be in a better and better position to take real and definitive action in the battle against boredom. In the next chapter we'll explore some of the many gambits open to you once you've completed your reconnaissance, made your battle plans and readied yourself to plunge into action.

8 *Taking the Plunge: Sample Solutions*

Foam "Iceberg" Startles the Aussies

SYDNEY (UPI)—Thousands of Australians—victims of an April Fool's Day prank—gaped as electronics millionaire Dick Smith sailed into Sydney harbor towing a giant "iceberg."

With a radio reporter broadcasting live from the "iceberg," Smith fooled harborside watchers, radio listeners and newsmen rushing to cover the event as he came slowly into sight.

The "iceberg" was a barge covered with white plastic sheets and fire-fighting foam. In the gloom and drizzle of early dawn it looked like the real thing.

Radio and TV stations and newspaper offices were swamped with calls. Scores of small craft raced in to inspect the strange object. Ferry skippers politely got out of the way.

Smith told radio listeners he planned to moor the "iceberg" near the Opera House so it could be cut up into tiny cubes—to be sold at 10 cents each as "Dicksicles."

"The prank cost me $1,450," he said. "I do these things for kicks . . . takes the boredom out of everyday work."

—United Press International, April 2, 1978

"A lot of people enjoy being dead but they're not dead really, they're just backing away from life. Reach out, take a chance, get hurt even, play as well

Up From Boredom, Down From Fear

as you can. GO TEAM. . . . GO. Gimme an L.
Gimme an I. Gimme a V. Gimme an E. L.I.V.E!
LIVE! Otherwise you got nothing to talk about in the
locker room. . . ."

—Maude in *Harold & Maude*

You can talk yourself blue in the face. You
can tally your test scores and ponder the results. You can
list, catalogue and classify your each and every yawn. But
none of it's going to do a damn bit of good unless you're
prepared to get out there and *do* something.

Floating foam icebergs may not be your style. Fourteen
hundred and fifty dollars may not be your price. Granted,
pranks and practical jokes won't see you through a long,
lonely winter. But it's not *what* you do, it's *whether* you do
anything at all. In general, when it comes to making decisions and taking action, we tend to err on the conservative
side. Jean-Paul Sartre, in an interview, observed: "Naturally, in the course of my life I have made lots of mistakes,
large and small, for one reason or another, but at the heart
of it all, every time I made a mistake it was because I was
not radical enough." So when in doubt, a good rule to follow is: Always take the side of change. Your resources are
limited only by the outer reaches of your imagination. You
need to make a commitment, true. But it doesn't have to be
financial. You know now how you'd like to lead your life
and you've got the tools to do it. Making it happen, though,
means promising yourself to be loyal to the part of you that
seeks adventure, that loves the unknown, that wants to
live.

The solutions that follow are just some of the productive
ways to take action on your own behalf. I'm sure you'll be
able to come up with many more. . . .

The Periodic Purge

How many times have you wondered why you continue to play bridge even though you think it's a waste of time? Or why you don't cancel your subscription to *The New Yorker* since you never have the time to read it? Or why you play the tuba every Friday night with your old college chums, even though you hate the tuba and the common thread of your early days together has long since frayed? Or why you do any of a million and one things you no longer actively enjoy?

Habit. Pure and simple. Once you establish a pattern, it's easier to go with it than to stop. That's fine when the habit is something you want to hang onto for a lifetime, like brushing your teeth. But when it comes to friends, possessions and commitments, unexamined habits generally contain a lot of deadwood. Now deadwood may be a ruthless way to refer to your old next-door neighbor of twenty years, but if he habitually chews your ear off for an hour and a half every time you run into each other, while you eye the nearest exit, he's got to go. If you've dragged your childhood stamp collection from one end of the country to the other, not because it's worth something or you still have an interest in stamps, but because you never thought of doing anything else, get rid of it and start a new hobby. If you still go to monthly meetings of the historical society, even though you inevitably fall asleep, look for a new channel for your civic pride.

The periodic purge is a chance to reassess the priorities in your life, then purge or demote those you no longer enjoy and promote those you haven't fully explored.

Keith was used to thinking of Tom as his best friend. After all, they'd known each other since junior high. Tom had

231

sort of adopted him as a little brother. They were the same age but Tom was brawny, a football player, while Keith was a scrawny intellectual gadfly. They'd never had much in common, but there was a lot of mutual affection and respect. In time they went their separate ways professionally, but every month they got together for dinner. At first Keith had welcomed this tradition as a sign that his life, no matter how chaotic, still had continuity. But as he made new friends and developed new interests, it began to seem a burden. He found himself resenting the times with Tom. He was bored by the endless reminiscences, the pointless nostalgia; there were other things he'd rather be doing. But it never occurred to him to consider that he might be suffering from relationship boredom. So their friendship, once so important to both of them, deteriorated into empty gestures and meaningless rituals.

If Keith had realized what was going on, he could have taken steps to ensure the preservation of the positive aspects of their friendship while minimizing his boredom. For, given their divergent paths, they were simply putting too many demands on each other.

Were Keith to practice the *periodic purge*, he would probably decide to see Tom once every few months rather than once a week. Tom, in effect, would have been demoted from "best friend" status to "one of my old buddies." This would clear the field for new friends who might have more to offer Keith at this time in his life, but it also would save what's left of his friendship with Tom. To do less would imply that force of habit was the only cement holding them together, which would be insulting, condescending and untrue.

The *periodic purge* can also minimize the everyday boredom of grocery shopping, routine office work, ironing, gardening—all those tasks you do on a regular basis but don't really enjoy. If the supermarket bores you, either do your shopping all at once and less frequently, pay a little more and have your groceries delivered, or try a different market every few weeks. If you hate to file, but like to type, you may be able to trade tasks with someone of the opposite persuasion. If it's ironing that drives you wild, throw out your 100-percent cottons and remember next time to buy permanent press. The principle, in other words, is to drop the task altogether if you can. If you can't, either do it differently or less often.

Where friends are concerned, take a little time to examine whom you enjoy the most, and whom you spend your time with. Often you'll find the two do not coincide. Or activities. Do you spend most of your leisure time doing those things you most enjoy? Probably not. Tastes change as we grow and develop new interests, but our patterns often fail to reflect these changes.

Next time you're invited to dinner or a party, stop and think about whether that's how you really want to spend Saturday night. If not, say no. You don't have to give a reason. Often, boredom comes from abdicating control, from letting others dictate the content and rhythm of one's days. We're either too lazy or afraid, in other words, to examine our priorities carefully and then act to bring our lives more closely into line with our values.

Practice limiting your relationships to those areas that aren't boring. If Frank is a great fishing companion but not so good at making conversation, don't invite him to your next dinner party. It doesn't have to be all or nothing.

It's not always possible, of course, to alter or banish everyone or everything that bores you. Your wife may talk about her job in more detail than you'd like. Whereas she may find your obsession with jogging less than riveting. That doesn't necessarily mean you should purge your mate. Or you may find one another increasingly predictable in bed. Chastity is clearly not the only answer. And what about your boss? She may drone on and on about the last staff meeting, but you can't very well avoid her without risking your job. In cases like these, try exploring new areas of the other person's physical or mental landscape. Your boss may have a rich and unplumbed fantasy life, or a childhood that no one's ever wondered about. Getting away from labels—boss, mother-in-law, brother, daughter, etcetera—frees up a lot of areas for questioning that are otherwise off limits.

Where your spouse is concerned, drop the idea that you "should" be interested in his or her every move. Don't be afraid to admit you're bored. And don't panic. All human beings are inherently interesting. A few bland patches in a relationship are just indicators of the places fear is keeping you from exploring further. Take sex. Here's an area where we're all afraid. No one feels attractive enough, big enough, small enough, often enough, long enough, or whatever. Sex, therefore, is particularly susceptible to boredom, for our feelings of inadequacy lead us to limit our sexual behavior to a very safe, narrow range. Having sex more or less frequently, changing positions and locations, talking about your fantasies or what you find erotic—small changes can make a big difference. Moreover, they can open up the kind of communication between you that leads to bigger changes.

The Binge

Breakfast in bed, a shopping spree, a night on the town—the therapeutic effects of a little self-indulgence are well-known. Abstinence, too, can be exhilarating. Remember when you quit smoking or went on a crash diet? Times like these give intensity to everyday life, for *conscious change of any kind brings in its wake an acute awareness of the presence and power of the Sane Me.* And boredom cannot coexist with a heightened sense of one's own sanity.

Chris is vibrant and curious and loves adventure. We've been friends for years, and it never occurred to me that she might be bored. Most of the time she isn't. But recently she confessed that she finds sex so dull that it's become more trouble than it's worth.

Now twenty-eight, Chris was a virgin until two years ago. Bill, her first "serious" boyfriend, was the only person she'd ever slept with. When they broke up, Chris found herself wondering whether she wanted to get involved with another man or not. Maybe she just wasn't very sexy. It hadn't occurred to her that she could apply the same energy and interest she brought to the rest of her life to sex. In her family it simply wasn't discussed. Sex was in a category all by itself, and Chris unwittingly had internalized this attitude. So instead of subjecting her sexual mores to the same close scrutiny that led her to adopt her own values in other areas, they remained unexamined. And dull. "Nice girls don't sleep around. . . ." "You'll get a bad reputation. . . ." "Women aren't supposed to like it. . . ." Once Chris verbalized some of these beliefs she was amazed by her own conservatism. "That doesn't sound like me!" she exclaimed. And, indeed, it wasn't. Rather, it was those voices from the past, the Prosecuting Attorney and the Prophet of Doom, up to their old tricks—convincing Chris that the safest, most conventional route was the best. And fear-induced boredom was the result.

I suggested that Chris try a version of the *binge*, while suspending judgment on sex altogether until she'd collected more information on her own reactions. Chris tried my ideas, went out with a lot of different men, slept with those she found attractive, and took mental notes on who and what she liked, didn't like and why. I'd also asked her to stand back a bit and take a lighter view of any sexual encounter—to try looking at sex as fun, interesting, entertaining, a learning experience rather than a life commitment.

A few months later Chris phoned to say she was actually starting to look forward to sex. She'd realized that her boredom stemmed from feelings and beliefs that were quite irrational. She'd first slept with Bill because she thought they would probably get married. But as soon as she sensed that their relationship was going nowhere, she'd shut down, since sex, according to her Prosecuting Attorney, was only for married couples. After they split up her Prophet of Doom convinced her that sex with anyone else would lead to some pretty awful consequences—social ostracism, VD, being loved-for-her-body-not-her-mind, and assorted other overblown fears. When this didn't happen Chris was able to see sex as just another aspect of life—something to be explored and enjoyed.

The *binge* is a good way of shaking yourself out of physical and mental ruts. If you spend most of your time doing things for other people, give yourself a week of total self-indulgence. If that's not possible, set aside an hour a day for yourself—just you and nobody else. Or see how little money you can spend for a week and then blow what you've saved on an "extravagance" for you or someone you love. If you're a workhorse and tired of it, see what happens if you stop—not slow down—STOP. The *binge* is extreme: It requires that you abandon your preconceptions, throw yourself into something you'd like to explore further and see where it takes you.

236

The Grand Illusion

If "all the world's a stage and all the men and women merely players," then it behooves us to play our parts with flair, imagination and verve. Viewing life as theater is particularly liberating because it opens up the possibility of playing a variety of different roles.

Too often we get trapped by our own myopia. This leads to reactions like these: "I'm not athletic"; "I don't understand modern art"; "Intelligent people don't do that"—limiting, negative ways of looking at life's possibilities. So what if you're smart? You can still go bowling and have a good time. You don't have to join a league, swill beer and fall into someone else's stereotype. Or maybe you don't really see the point of many of the paintings being shown today. Modern art covers a lot of territory—from photography to happenings and street theater. As do sports—t'ai chi or jogging, for instance, call for very different skills and temperaments than football.

Looking at yourself as constantly changing, adapting and growing keeps you from getting entrenched in a single self-image. Taking on new roles can help you find your next direction.

Paul is a well-known architect in southern California. He teaches part-time, likes his work, designed his own home, and adores his wife and daughter. He's quite content with things just the way they are—most of the time. But every once in a while Paul tires of this idyll. He gets a twinge of life-style boredom. He wants excitement, maybe even a little danger. It used to be that he'd ignore this feeling when it washed over him. And it did recede again, but always Paul felt slightly cheated afterward, and more than a little depressed.

237

When we talked about this sensation I asked Paul why he didn't just go out and take some risks, give himself a little slack to explore. Turns out he'd had a very unsettled childhood. Most of his youth was spent dreaming up a secure, foolproof life for himself, and he was still amazed that it had all come true. Now he hesitated to rock the boat for fear it would vanish. I suggested he try giving it a little jiggle just to see what would happen.

Because of his strong professional identity, Paul tended to meet mostly people in related fields. And he talked architecture constantly, regardless of his audience. For starters, I said, try giving people different information about yourself. Instead of the same old spiel when someone asks what you do, tell them something besides "I'm an architect." Tell them something more revealing, more personal, or even make something up.

Paul was skeptical, but said he'd try it. Later, he told me it was much harder to do than he'd thought. It was difficult to let go of even a little bit of his hard-won identity. His first success was at a cocktail party. He met a sailboat enthusiast and, on the spur of the moment, gave himself a seafaring grandparent. They spent the evening talking boats instead of architecture and Paul went sailing the next weekend.

From there I encouraged him to try other flights of fancy. What would you be doing . . . if you'd never gone to college . . . if you'd never met your wife . . . if you could change your identity at will?

As a result of thinking about himself in new ways Paul began to feel and act much looser. And he discovered, by giving his imagination free rein, that there were lots of things he enjoyed doing that added variety and richness to his life. *The imagination is a powerful tool. When coupled with action, it can always lead you out of boredom.*

238

Taking the Plunge: Sample Solutions

Let's look at one of momentary boredom's favorite breeding grounds—waiting. You can either wait alone or with others. Say you're feeling antisocial and you're fifth in line at the supermarket check-out stand. There's plenty of fantasy material in all those shopping carts. Create an unexpected life for your fellow shoppers, based solely on the contents of their baskets. Is all that Cool Whip really for the kids, or have you cracked a ring of suburban swingers? Remember, no one can see what you're thinking.

If you're in a sociable mood, you are in an even better position to play with reality. These are some of the ways I've found that work best:

> *Spread-a-Rumor*—In the thirties, when Orson Welles broadcast the *War of the Worlds* and convinced millions of Americans that the aliens were invading, it may have been a night of terror, but I'm willing to bet that no one within earshot of a radio was bored. Not that I'm suggesting you terrorize your friends and neighbors. But a few small speculations on the truth behind the news can keep you all in a state of suspense for hours.

> *New Identities*—Relating to strangers in new ways—as a tightrope walker, dog catcher, novelist—not only opens up new vistas on others' psyches, but provides a lot of interesting information on your own. You may find out some things about yourself that will lead to bigger changes. Try doing something that seems out of character for someone of your age, intelligence or social sophistication.

> *White Lies*—Don't let the truth fence you in. If your stories don't seem to sparkle,

239

improve on them. If your life story lacks pizzazz throw some in. You're not hurting anybody and, at the very least, you'll find yourself more entertaining.

Social Experiments—Spend a day focusing
on a single premise or objective and apply it
to all the situations you encounter. You might
decide that you're going to find out what everyone you meet had for breakfast, what they
think about the Middle East or whether
they've ever contemplated disappearing. Or
you might decide to approach people with the
idea that everyone has lovable qualities and
you're going to find at least one in every person you meet that day.

Dress and personal style is another area that succumbs
to boredom easily—especially as people get older. We've
all seen the sixty-year-old woman who still sports the same
hair-do and makeup she wore forty years ago. Lest you get
stuck in your own fashion backwater, try on some new costumes:

—Buy an outfit that's "not you," something
that personifies a look you admire but don't
think you can quite carry off.

—Dress inappropriately sometimes—wear
your opera cape to the airport or your jeans
to visit your great-aunt Sue.

—Splurge on a totally new hair style.

—Start or stop wearing makeup for a while or
get your face done by a pro.

240

Leap Before You Look

Jean-Paul Sartre once wrote a short story which concludes with the hero shooting at pedestrians from the window of his Paris apartment. He does not know his victims; indeed, it is the very fact of his estrangement from them that produces the impulse to pull the trigger. The man who goes berserk, who's "mad as hell and not gonna take it anymore," has almost become a staple of the nightly news. But impulsive activity can also be neutral. It need not necessarily endanger the welfare of society. It is neither inherently constructive nor destructive. Used creatively, however, it can be a reliable personal ally in combating boredom, for it goes against the cautious, indecisive behavior our fears have led us to believe is the only safe way of responding to the world. Most of us, after all, are not cold-blooded killers at heart—no matter how much permission we give ourselves to act on impulse. Approached correctly, leaping before you look cures many more problems than it creates. One of these problems is boredom.

Boredom arises in part from the stamping of patterns onto our consciousness. Three meals a day. Eight hours of sleep. The seventh-inning stretch. Up to a point, these may be trite if true ways of coping with periodic hunger or fatigue. It is infinitely easier, for instance, to tell a child that he must eat three balanced meals a day than to explain that seventy grams of protein a day in combination with so many grams of carbohydrates and so forth are needed to sustain a body of so many pounds under such and such an environment. But when the pattern becomes onerous— when your Sane Me doesn't feel like eating simply because it's twelve noon—then it's high time to break out.

An arbitrary choice, a decision to act in a different man-

ner than you have ever done before, can free you from the
bonds of boredom.

Margaret had always thought of herself as a responsible, law-abiding woman. An on-time woman. A woman who had life very much in the palm of her hand. Every morning at eight-thirty sharp she left the house and drove to the clinic where she was a medical secretary. Every afternoon at five P.M. she drove home. She always took the same route. After twenty-five years she knew every bump and bush on the road. One evening she came to a familiar intersection. The light had just turned green and she was proceeding across at her usual pace when suddenly a car came out of nowhere and hit her broadside. The car was demolished but, miraculously, Margaret wasn't hurt, just shaken. I was almost killed! she thought. And suddenly the world looked very different. The trees were greener, the flowers brighter, and Margaret felt wide awake for the first time in years. When she finally made it home she absent-mindedly prepared the supper she'd planned the day before—ham, lima beans and a salad. It was basically the same supper she had every Thursday night, with minor variations. Sometimes she had corn instead of lima beans, or she added a little pineapple to the ham. And as she munched, she thought.

It was clear that some changes were in order. She'd gradually become an automaton. She went to work, kept the house and waited for her husband to notice her. He traveled a lot, and when he was home he was either out cycling or working on his bicycle—an enthusiasm that left Margaret cold. Their daughter was off at school and, except for frequent collect phone calls, didn't need her mother anymore. So her free time was really her own. But she'd forgotten how to use it. There was a time, when she was a girl, when each day seemed full of promise, but not anymore.

242

Margaret's life-style boredom had snuck up on her gradually, but once she recognized it she decided to do something about it.

Margaret came to see me expecting, I think, a traditional Freudian analysis—a solution that would dredge her soul. Instead, I asked her to think of something she could change in her home environment. Her first thought had to do with food. She had a big collection of cookbooks, but still she made the same old things night after night. Often, she said, she was too tired to start from scratch. I suggested that next time she went shopping, she pick some prepared foods at random from the shelves—foods she'd never eaten before—and try them. Her second thought had to do with the swimming pool. Since her daughter had left home no one used it. Margaret knew she needed the exercise, but instead she usually ended up in front of the television. "How about inviting others to join you?" I asked. "That way you'd be committed in advance, and you might make some new friends as well. Try asking people you wouldn't ordinarily think of socializing with."

Margaret experimented with a number of variations on the "leap before you look" technique, and enough of them worked to start her life moving in a different direction. Now she has her own group of friends, she's started taking some classes at night, and she no longer resents her husband and child for having their own lives.

The essence of *leap before you look* is impulsive action. If you can't think of something to do, do something before you have a chance to talk yourself out of it. It's about the only way there is to overcome inertia, for the act itself creates the momentum you need to carry you forward.

These are some sample activities that have worked for me:

Up From Boredom, Down From Fear

—On a free afternoon or evening, open your address book, pick a name at random and invite that person out for a drink.

—Follow a stranger. Playing detective is not only engrossing in itself, but you'll end up seeing places and doing things outside your daily experience just because our lives generally follow the same beaten paths day after day.

—Frequent shops, restaurants and neighborhoods you know nothing about. The yellow pages are a great resource when you're bored. Just let your finger fall where it may, and then check out the consequences.

—Ask a travel agent to make a list of all the places you could go for the amount you're prepared to spend on your vacation. Then put the possible destinations in a hat, draw one and stick to it.

—Make a list of things you'd never do, pick one at random and do it wholeheartedly. This way you don't get trapped in the decision-making process at the expense of taking action.

—Bestow your free will on a friend for a day and let him or her make all the decisions. It will help you uncover the rigidities in yourself that keep you from being open to change.

Mary, Mary, Quite Contrary

No matter how satisfactory or beneficial they may be, situations that go on and on indefinitely have an insidious way of becoming boring. This "hidden" boredom is not only difficult to perceive, it's damn near impossible to shake. Or so it would seem. You are happy, after all, doing what you want at last. But what does this really mean? Let's start with the word. "Happiness" is one of those pie-in-the-sky words, like "freedom," "truth," "beauty" and "love." It evaporates because it evokes everything and nothing at the same time. If every automobile in the world were painted red, there would be no such things as a "red automobile." To be happy infers a similarly generalized state of being. It reveals, as Mae West once said, "less than meets the eye." Pie-in-the-sky words also tend to be eternal. What is true will always be true. What's beautiful today will be beautiful tomorrow. The love of my life. They lived happily ever after. No self-respecting fairytale ever ends with the prince and princess living *more or less* happily ever after. They simply move forward like love-struck pawns, arm and arm into the sunset.

Given all the pessimism and catastrophy generated by the twentieth century, one might suppose that idyllic situations would be as rare as hens' teeth. Far from it. There are those, believe it or not, who deliberately set out to become hog farmers or prizefighters or fashion illustrators, people who are not merely good at what they do, but who don't look back on their lives with regret. They do become bored, however, Bored by success. Bored by winning. Bored by knowing the consequence of their behavior in advance.

Summoning the courage to act in a manner contrary to

what you have always done in the past—even acting against what you perceive to be your own best interest—can lead you out of boredom and back to sanity.

Steve and Joanne had read all the marriage manuals. They dutifully made love several times a week in a variety of positions. They didn't confine sex to the bedroom, nor did they always choose the same time of day. Steve had been known to bring home exotic oils and hand-sewn lingerie for Joanne. She in turn bought him a dozen pairs of multicolored briefs and a Japanese kimono. It was all according to life as it is lived in one of the trendier magazines for young marrieds. So why should they be bored?

They had come to my office for a consultation and it seemed quite clear that it was not their relationship that was in trouble. Rather, they had gotten stuck in a life style that they thought they should be enjoying, but in fact were finding very unrewarding. I told them to try turning their usual patterns upside down as a way of shaking up the habits they'd acquired.

First, they were to abstain from all dutiful sex. If they really wanted it, they were to confine their intercourse to the missionary position at night in bed. Their leisure time they usually spent together, bicycling, jogging, going to the movies. I suggested they both spend more time alone, either working or doing things they hadn't done for a long time.

When they returned the following week, they were both eager to report on the insights they had gained from their experiment. First of all, they had a renewed interest in sex. Joanne didn't like being constrained to the missionary position, but she'd discovered that knowing they weren't going to make love during the day freed her to concentrate on other things. Steve liked the sense he had that he didn't have to perform if he didn't feel like it. Essentially, they'd gotten back in touch with their own personal sexual rhythms—knowledge that was lost to them when they'd listened to others' ideas of when, how and what they "ought" to be doing. As for the rest of their lives, they both agreed they were relieved to give up jogging, but they missed cycling together. In his time alone Steve realized how much he enjoys his work—he's a free-lance writer—and has resolved to spend some of his leisure writing for his own pleasure. Joanne found she'd cut herself off from the company of friends she enjoyed, just because she thought she and Steve "should" spend more time together. With all this information on hand, Steve and Joanne are now in a position to decide on the kinds of changes they want to make in their lives.

When things start to go stale for me I've developed a technique I call Plan/Counterplan. If there's a weekend coming up that I'm not really looking forward to I review what's on tap, even write out my schedule, and then completely reverse it. If I'd planned to sleep till noon and then listen to the ball game, I might get up at the crack of dawn and go fishing. Instead of dinner and a movie on Saturday night, I might either stay home or visit friends—and so forth.

This technique can be applied to every aspect of your life and, basically, involves going against the grain of established patterns of behavior. It's bound to feel uncomfortable at first, but you'll learn so much about your real needs and directions that you'll find it well worth the initial effort.

Try it out on a small scale first:

> —If you always drive to work and take the same route every day, change your mode of transportation, or find a new way to get there—even if it takes longer.

—If you love science fiction, switch to detective novels for a while. Stop reading the magazines you subscribe to and buy some you've never read before. Try reading the stories you usually skip in the newspaper. If they still don't interest you, think about what others might be getting out of them.

—Go to movies you'd ordinarily veto. Try a matinee if you always go at night. If you've never walked out on a boring film, do it now.

—Change your sleeping schedule. Find out what goes on around you at four A.M. As long as you get your six to eight hours in somewhere you'll be fine.

The Grass Is Always Greener

It has always struck me as peculiar that people tend to be dissatisfied with themselves, that they are jealous of one another's circumstances, that they covet each other's wives or husbands or Maseratis—and yet almost never do anything about it.

While discontent is endemic to all industrial societies (including Third World nations which are striving for industrial status), the gap between "wanting" and "having" appears only to grow wider with increased production. Our lack, in other words, is not so much material as it is spiritual: a Great Dane or a color television or another hundred shares of IBM will have but a limited effect on desire. To retreat into a cave, however, strikes me as equally peculiar, since it flies in the face of five thousand years of accumulated wisdom. Fortunately, there is a more expedient alternative: *You can let your own desires teach you who you are.* You can explore your fantasies publicly, without shame, and even if they are impossible to duplicate there are many positive and creative ways to bring what's inside you out into the open air.

Living in someone else's shoes will either give you some new ideas or help you look at what you've got from a new perspective.

The Jacobs, old college friends of mine, moved to California about five years ago. They've lived in Hollywood ever since, close to Joe's job, but right in the middle of the smog belt. And every summer it's the same old story: As soon as the heat rolls in and the smog starts to build, the complaints begin. "It's too smoggy to do anything. L.A. is such a bore." And they continue until the weather clears. The Jacobs are always talking about moving to the beach, but they never do anything about it.

Jill and Bob, native Californians, live right on the ocean but they both work in town. And they hate the commute. "What's the point of living at the beach if you have to spend hours sitting on the freeway twiddling your thumbs and inhaling other people's exhaust fumes? Why, I remember when Los Angeles was nothing but orange groves and eucalyptus trees."

Two classic cases of situational boredom, right? I got these couples together, thinking they were perfect candidates for *the grass is always greener.* Why not trade houses during the week? That way the Jacobs could enjoy the ocean breezes and spend weekends in town when the smog was lighter. Jill and Bob could avoid the rush-hour traffic and still spend time on the beach. Their first reaction to my suggestion was horror. We couldn't do that. It would be so disruptive. As they talked, though, the obstacles became less apparent and they decided to try it out for a short time.

At the end of the trial period we met for dinner to compare reactions. The Jacobs sheepishly confessed that they couldn't stand the beach. It was damp and foggy and there was nothing to do but swim and breathe the fresh air. They looked forward to returning to the hustle and bustle, if not the smog, of the city. Jill and Bob, on the other hand, had had a wonderful time. They loved being closer to their jobs and were hoping to be able to move to town, keeping their beachhouse for weekends.

Not all swaps work out quite so smoothly. You may want out long before your time is up. But they are always instructive. I spoke to someone who'd traded houses and children with a friend for the weekend, only to find she was allergic to down pillows, couldn't sleep on a water bed, and the children watched cartoons all Saturday morning—a practice she abhors. When she returned home Sunday night it was with renewed appreciation for her own environs.

The grass is always greener suggests that a change is not only as good as a rest—it's better. And it works on a variety of levels. The popularity of swap meets, garage sales and the like is proof enough that one person's junk is another's treasure. There's no reason not to apply the same principle to jobs, cities, even countries. How about exchanging tastes with someone who likes different music, books or food? Or you might think about trading boring habits—the contents of your liquor cabinet for a friend's TV set, with instructions not to return them. The variations are endless.

Changing the Rules

If there are indeed intelligent life forms in outer space, and if those forms should ever decide to take a tour of the earth, they would undoubtedly come away more confused than enlightened. They would discover, for example, that in America the traditional color of a bride's gown is white, while in China it is black; that in India cows are treated with reverence, while in Argentina those same cows are regularly ground up into hamburger. Everywhere they went they would see that social rules are different—and for no apparent reason.

Rules are made to modify behavior. Sometimes this modification benefits society at large (thou shalt not kill), sometimes it benefits a few (thou shall be on time to work) and sometimes it benefits no one (thou shalt not mention certain topics at the dinner table). Rules are also artificial: people make rules, just as they make bricks or bottles or mousetraps. When rules interdict the natural, rational flow of ideas (don't discuss sex, religion or politics in mixed company, for instance) they are counterproductive and need to be swept aside—otherwise frustration and boredom inevitably result. Changing the rules, of course, presupposes knowing what the rules are. And oftentimes rules go unspoken (don't ask too many questions, avoid controversy, be polite). Walking into a situation full of unspoken rules is rather like walking into an emotional mine field—the safest thing to do is freeze—which is exactly what happens at cocktail parties, awards ceremonies and so on.

By changing or eliminating the rules you can explore in a boredom-free environment.

Rebecca and David are a very popular young couple. Active, bright, engaged in living examined and creative lives, they naturally attract other people. When they were first married they loved having lots of friends. As time wore on, however, the circle widened until they both had so many social commitments there was little time left to be alone together. The solution, they thought, would be to have evenings "at home" once a week. It would give them a

251

chance to see everyone and they would also have more time alone.

At first the evenings were fun. More like parties than spending time talking or doing things with friends, but they did seem to be fulfilling their purpose. After a few weeks, though, things went flat. When David and Rebecca sat down to figure out what was going on they realized that, instead of the intimacies, self-revelations and doubts they used to exchange with people, their social interaction had become very superficial. Being with a large group of people had imposed inhibitions and constraints they hadn't anticipated. The result was fear-induced boredom.

They decided to change the rules. One week they asked everyone to tell a secret about themselves. Another they suggested people talk only with people they didn't know very well. And they brought up subjects they'd been thinking about and asked everyone to join in a discussion. The evenings began to have a focus, a purpose beyond exchanging gossip and polite talk. Their friends started to participate more, suggesting ideas and new rules themselves. Soon the inhibitions, fears and conventions that make most social functions so boring dropped away.

Changing the rules can be applied to a variety of human relationships. All that's required is to step back long enough to see what unwritten conventions you're subscribing to, and then consciously choose new modes of interacting. The relationship between parents and their grown children, for instance, often profits from this sort of examination. All too frequently the rules set down during childhood remain in effect long after they've become obsolete.

Couples who've worked out a comfortable routine of who does what when often find the routine becoming a tyranny. Laundry on Monday, ironing on Tuesday, dinner out on Friday night. Why? If there's no particular reason, change the rules. And what about all the unspoken contracts we make with one another to keep the lid on certain taboo areas, such as "I won't talk about your overeating if you'll stop complaining about my mother" and so on. Looking objectively at what areas in your relationship are no longer open to negotiation will provide you with a lot of challenging material to work with.

Make War

"War," as von Clausewitz defined it succinctly in his nineteenth-century treatise on the subject, "is diplomacy by other means." But it is more than that. The prospect of confrontation, especially when it's face to face, stirs up a whole raft of emotions in every individual— most of them based on fear. Partly we're afraid of being hurt, partly of losing, but mostly that, win or lose, it won't be worth it.

It won't do any good to take on City Hall, we say. The world has grown too complex. And, when it comes to personal contact, we are too dependent on one another to risk it all with a display of anger. True, true. Ralph Nader notwithstanding, one angry individual usually doesn't put much of a dent in the bureaucratic machine. Nor does one angry woman a movement make. But somewhere, at some point, we all have to put our feet down, so to speak. Some people are slow to anger, others have a short fuse. But whatever your own tolerance level may be, if you pass it without making a fuss, if you just let it smolder, it leads straight to frustration and thence to boredom.

Relationships get dull because people avoid confrontation.

Before Jan and Jerry got married political differences

were one of the staples of their conversations. She was an ardent feminist; he believed in equal pay for equal work, but thought the rest of her rhetoric was sour grapes. He was a staunch Zionist; Jan's sympathies lay with the Palestinians. She wanted no part of a government that could promote the war in Vietnam; he thought he could work for change within the system. Why did they get married at all, you may wonder. Largely because they both loved to talk.

After the first year or so of their marriage things started to change between them. Not that either one of them was convinced by the other, but their differences went underground. They'd bought a house they couldn't really afford and had a lot of financial worries. Jan was pregnant and Jerry didn't want to upset her. Bit by bit a pattern formed. And by the time they'd been together several years, you'd never guess they'd ever talked about anything more substantial than the latest car-repair bill. And it wasn't just social issues that weren't discussed—personal grudges, resentments and minor injustices were also allowed to fester. When they thought about it at all, it was hard to remember the intensity of those early days. We're just too busy for that sort of thing now, they would say. The truth was that they had grown dependent on one another and were afraid to rock the boat; in addition, their image of the ideal marriage allowed no room for conflict. A disagreement among friends was one thing, but between husband and wife it meant there was something very wrong. Consequently, though Jan and Jerry were a picture of happiness from the outside, on the inside they were seething. And when they weren't seething, they were bored.

Clearly, they needed a refresher couse in *making war*. I suggested they practice fighting. "Set aside some time each day," I said, "to bring up recent irritations. And if you have none you can always watch the news together and

254

talk about it afterwards!'' The results were startling. Most of their friends were sure they were witnessing the end of another marriage. Their children didn't know what to make of it all, but they were fascinated. Their parents suddenly seemed to disagree on everything, but they were talking to each other and were happier than they'd been in ages.

Jan and Jerry, like many of us, had lost confidence in the innate strength of their relationship. What brought them together initially was what would hold them together in the long run. If they could just recover it. Many times a relationship fails, not because it hasn't got a lot going for it, but because the participants are afraid to keep testing and stretching its limits. Again, by cutting your risks, you actually increase them.

Making war works best when both sides are open and honest and—most important—retain their sense of humor. It can work for you on the job, with relatives and friends and, probably, with those you live with. Next time you're tempted to compromise, to bite your tongue, to keep the peace, consider the consequences. If one of them is boredom, *make war*.

When All Else Fails

Not long ago, a Catholic divinity student took a month off from his studies to meditate at a Zen retreat south of San Francisco. There the monks put him through a rigorous drill: he rose promptly at four A.M., meditated three times a day, three and a half hours at a stretch, ate three spartan meals, worked in the kitchen, washed, and went to bed by nine P.M.—all without uttering a word. Upon his return to college, a professor asked him how it had gone. "Terrific," replied the student, beaming. "I wasn't bored for a second." "Oh, I'm so sorry," said the professor. "You see, that was exactly what was supposed to happen."

We're so used to categorizing boredom as a feeling to be avoided that it's hard to remember that it can be a great teacher. So if you've tried everything and you're still bored, relax. Accept it. You're very likely on the verge of something new.

Boredom is often a herald of change and can be observed as an intriguing and interesting phenomenon in its own right.

Quince is a private investigator. He does occasional undercover work for businesses whose employees are dipping too deeply into the till. He tracks down husbands and wives. In his younger days, Quince was a police detective in Manhattan. "Lots of murders, rapes, armed robberies back then," he reminisces. "Never a dull moment, if you know what I mean."

Since he quit the force and moved to California three years ago, Quince has pretty much confined himself to paper chases. But until recently he always had a story to tell about the oddballs who rolled through his office. Lately, though, he hasn't been talking much about his work, nor about anything else for that matter. When I finally asked him why, Quince confessed with some bewilderment that he was tired of it all.

"I still think it's the most exciting job in the world. But all these people with their problems are starting to give me the creeps. I don't care what happens to them anymore. I must be getting old and calloused."

When I suggested this form of life-style boredom might be a natural reaction to twenty years of doing pretty much the same thing, Quince rejected the idea out of hand.

"If you could be anything in the world," I persisted, "besides an investigator, what would it be?"

"I don't know," he replied. "I've never done anything else."

Quince was bored with being a cop, and he simply couldn't admit it. After all, he's carried around one badge or another now for twenty years of his life. Twenty years is a long time to write off just like that.

I encouraged him to relax and think about it—not to quit his job, not to change his habits, *not to do anything*—just realize that he was temporarily becalmed and know that sooner or later it would pass.

After a few weeks Quince dropped by to tell me he'd been hired as a consultant by one of the film studios in town. They were shooting a movie on what it's *really* like to be a private eye. He was thrilled to be on the set joking with stars he never thought he'd see in person. "You know," he confided, "I think I was just bored with doing the same old thing day after day. But if I hadn't gotten bored, I'd never have gotten up the nerve to look for something new."

With the knowledge you now have, you probably won't ever find yourself in Quince's position. When you're feeling down, apathetic, indifferent, you'll have a pretty good idea of the reasons why. But that doesn't mean you'll always be able to do something about it right away. It doesn't hurt to try, of course, but if nothing seems to work, relax. Don't take your predicament too seriously. Wait and live with your boredom for a little while.

There may, in fact, be nothing that needs changing. You may have a case of stress-symptom boredom. You may just need a rest. Enthusiasm, even for the things we love most, has its natural cycles. It ebbs and flows and some-

257

times it's important to recognize that fact and go with it. Remember the importance of timing, and stay away from familiar people and activities for a while.

If none of this helps, it's very likely that the boredom you feel is a sign of growth—a portent of major changes that are in the works, but haven't quite surfaced yet. Think of it as a prelude rather than a wasteland—a chance to look within and learn.

Handy Hints

To finish off, here's an assortment of techniques to get you going when inspiration runs dry.

Situational Boredom

—Isolation of the Worst

Figure out which chores and obligations you really detest, then set aside a particular time each day or week to do them, so you don't have to carry them around with you the rest of the time.

—The Buddy System

Pair up with a friend and give each other the support and encouragement you need to get through boring jobs that can't be avoided. If you're lucky, your friend may not be bored by the same things you are, and you can switch.

258

Friendships

—Categorize your friends as to their age, sex, religion, social class, race and so forth and then make a determined effort to meet and mix with people in other categories.

—Work with a friend toward changing some part of your relationship that you don't enjoy.

—Explore other's ideas that you disagree with rather than avoiding "sensitive" issues. Don't judge. Just try to understand what they believe in and why.

Work

—Tune in or tune out of office politics.

—Ask for a different job at the same level.

—Investigate the possibility of temporary retirement, look for a new job or consider changing careers.

—Take a job that's more fun for less pay.

—Reorganize your schedule so as to change the sequence in which you do things.

—Find a new way to do something mundane.

Marriage

—Make an arrangement to listen to each other without interrupting for at least fifteen minutes.

—*Queen or King for a Night.* Give each other an hour, a night, or a weekend when one of you gets to have everything his or her own way sexually.

—Decide *not* to do something you would usually do on a

weekend—drive the car, watch TV or listen to music—and instead do something you've never done together before—go camping, get tickets for a boxing match or try roller-skating.

Children

—Refuse to take responsibility for your children's boredom. Place it back on their shoulders where it belongs. Parents' boredom is often the result of their efforts to "entertain" their children, when the best thing they could do for them is to encourage them to learn to entertain themselves.

Around the House

—Change the furniture around even though you like it the way it is.
—Paint your rooms different colors.
—Swap duties with the person you live with.
—Give something away.
—Learn how things work and how to fix them.
—Get a new kind of pet.

New Horizons

—Pick a Prejudice. Think of some activities or groups that your own stereotypes or biases have kept you from exploring and find out as much about them as you can through reading, the media and, most important, personal experience.

—Prepare for a second career by going to night school.

—Get a catalogue of the adult-education classes in your area and either pick a course you've always wanted to take or, if you can't decide, choose one at random. Send off your check before you can change your mind.

TV

—Bet on the outcome of any TV program—sporting events are the most likely prospects, but you can also bet on what's going to happen next in your favorite soap opera, sit com, or TV movie. Bet an amount you wouldn't feel bad about losing, but would feel good about winning. Or you can wager dinner, breakfast in bed, chores or sexual favors.

—Don't watch any of your favorite shows for a specified period of time.

—Buy a TV recorder and watch daytime shows at night or vice versa.

Parties

—Have an open house and invite everybody you know—regardless of whether you think they'll get along with anybody else there.

—Rent a bus and go somewhere.

—Make a movie with your friends, improvising costumes, makeup and script on the spot.

—Form a stimulation group with others who're interested in finding new ways to beat boredom.

Miscellany

—Scare yourself by doing something new and moderately frightening—like riding a roller coaster, asking a man for a date or going to your first punk rock concert.

—If you're clock conscious, get rid of all timepieces for a weekend.

—Tell someone off.

—Take half an hour or so to sit in a chair, close your eyes and listen to your mind work.

—Pick a noncompetitive physical goal—an eight-minute mile, twenty-five pushups or a long walk every day—and do it.

—Spend a weekend in which you stop any activity the minute you lose interest in doing it. Make a long list of things you can do in less than an hour and keep it handy for this occasion.

—If your schedule is very open, make lots of commitments. If it's very full, don't make any appointments for a day, a week, or a month.

Some of these solutions may sound like mere common sense, others may strike you as slightly silly, frivolous or shocking. Just reading them over and reacting won't do a thing for your boredom, however. Their essence lies not in the idea but in the experience. And only you can provide that for yourself. Action is the trigger that will catapult you up from boredom and down from fear.

9

Interesting People

Just as most fears are all in your head, and beauty is in the eye of the beholder, the capacity to charm, to delight, to be interesting to others, comes from within. It has very little to do with your occupation, your experience, your looks, age, race, social class or your talents. It does have to do with your behavior and your ideas and attitudes about yourself and the world. Boring people are rigid, conservative, locked up and imprisoned by their guilt and fear. They can make a trip to the moon sound like a drive to the drugstore—and vice versa. They can empty a roomful of people in the blink of an eye. But boring people are, above all, bored with their own lives. And their lack of enthusiasm, involvement and excitement not only dulls their own existence, it rubs off on others.

We all start out in life being inherently interesting. Put a baby in the middle of a crowded room and watch the focus of attention shift. Infants are so absorbing because their responses are so direct, so fresh, so uninhibited. The world for them is a constant source of wonder. They learn as naturally as they breathe. They are fearless, guiltless, totally themselves. But we are not babies. We are adults. And in the process of becoming adults we have learned not to stand on the coffee table, not to scream in restaurants and, inadvertently, not to be ourselves. The more *unlike* our original sane self we become, the more boring and bored we are.

Interesting people are not afraid to be themselves.

But what exactly does it mean to be "yourself"? Quite simply it means filtering out all the needless static that prevents us from sanely conducting our own lives on our own terms, that's what. It does not follow, however, that we must withdraw from the world and all its attendant stresses and strains. Rather, we can learn to see it as a challenge—a source of constant stimulation. Few of us would want to be hermits—even if we had the time or the discipline. We are not saints. Besides, a world without people wouldn't be much fun. But there are always going to be other voices out there telling us who's on first, what to wear, when we may take a giant step, where to dispose of our opinions, and why things are the way they are. Other voices—not your voice. As you've learned, however, once you know who you are, you can enlist the help of your Sane Me to assess and talk back to both your own Crazy Me and the crazies of others. You can forget about trying to please everybody else and start thinking about how to please yourself. No one is going to be interesting at all times to all people anyway, so you might as well be yourself and let the chips fall where they may (without being boorish, hostile or totally selfish and egocentric). The alternative—being something you're not—is clearly an abysmal prospect. Not only do you lose touch with your sane self, but you pay dearly for this loss in the inevitable boredom that follows.

Interesting people are not perfect. No one is. We all have problems. Interesting people have fears, anxieties and depressions just like the rest of us. They too can be insensitive, screw up, fail miserably and lose control. Beware of people who tell you they don't have any problems. They're either lying or, worse yet, they're unaware.

Interesting people are not super-gurus. They have no

particular monopoly on the world's wisdom. Their lives, in fact, are just as fraught with uncertainty as anyone else's. What then makes them different? For one thing, they're not afraid to admit their problems, and for another, they don't let them stand in their way. These differences are what give them their visible inner strength and power.

Interesting people know what their problems are. It's always easier in the short run to avoid thinking about the aspects of your life that give you trouble. Put a Band-Aid on it, we say. Ignore it and maybe it will go away. We feed on a diet of empty hopes instead of hard facts. But if you get scared at the thought of people talking behind your back, or the slightest self-indulgence makes you feel guilty, you've got a problem and you'd better face it. Otherwise your Prosecuting Attorney and Prophet of Doom will continue to thwart your every attempt to be yourself. Once you admit their existence, however, you can talk them right out of your way.

Interesting people know what their needs are. Once you get into the habit of being yourself, of doing what you really want to do, you'll start tuning in to what your needs really are. Interesting people, because they're not afraid to be themselves and to make mistakes, ultimately become familiar with their own needs. Part of this process is quite painful and scary since it involves experimenting with your life and trying out various possibilities until you find the ones that are right for you. If you're not frightened by this prospect, you have probably either worked out most of your boredom problems or you're so bored and apathetic you find it hard to imagine doing anything about it at all! The art of being excited involves walking that fine line between boredom and fear—getting the stimulation you need without scaring yourself to death, learning to come up from boredom and down from fear. If you're just starting along this road you'll need to spend time discovering just when you need stimulation, how much you need, and where you can get it but, believe me, the trip makes it all worthwhile.

Interesting people know how to meet their needs. Boring people are often bewildered people. They don't know what their needs are, nor how to meet them. They don't know what to do to turn themselves on. Interesting people know how to orchestrate their lives. When they're doing something that's about to pall, they know how to switch activities before the stimulation and interest are gone. They're free to drop what they are doing for greener pastures. If they've made a mistake they can quickly change course before it drags them down. They've learned that if they're taking risks, or juicing, and it's beginning to wear a little thin, maybe its time to turn to an egghead activity. Or they might want to lie back, relax, and get into the process of doing something simple, or switch to a goal-directed activity that has a low risk factor. By moving about freely from one activity to another, they don't burn out. Instead, they always have something to look forward to.

Interesting people take positions. Now, to "take a position" it is not necessary to go on a hunger strike to protest apartheid in South Africa. It need not have anything to do with politics, in fact. But it does have to do with taking risks, with laying yourself on the line. It means that you know who you are, what you need, and are willing to act on it. When there's a conflict between your needs, and the expectations, opinions or desires of others, give yourself the benefit of the doubt for a change. If you need a night away from your family, take it. If you disagree with your best friend, say so. Take a chance. Very often the enemies are in your own head. And if there is in fact a real conflict, better to have it out in the open than festering in the dark. Remember, you are conducting your life for your own benefit, not for the amusement or comfort of others.

Many of us shy away from taking a position simply because we prefer to live like ghosts; the less people know about me, we think, the less I am a target. This is not only untrue, but in many instances *it is your lack of position that makes you a tempting target.* Sure, it's scary to stand up and let everyone see you for what you are—especially if you've been·in hiding for years and years—but consider the alternative . . . certain and unending boredom.

A person who takes a position is merely someone who has thought about something long enough to reach an honest conclusion that he or she wants to share with others. Whether or not you adhere to that conclusion forever is not important. People are not so dissimilar to seasons after all. They change. Ideals come and go. "Anyone who isn't a communist by the time he's seventeen is an idiot," an astute political observer once said, "and anyone who's still a communist by the time he's thirty-seven is also an idiot." What matters is that you aren't deluding yourself at the time, that you choose to profess something because you believe in it, and not because you ought to believe in it.

Being yourself and taking a stand both imply that you've got your life pretty well in hand—and this is our next axiom:

Interesting people take control of their lives. This is not as difficult as it may at first appear. All of us exercise a modicum of control over our lives, whether we know it or not. Perhaps it is as simple as the brand of beer we choose at the market, or the color of our car, or deciding whether or not to walk around the corner and get a haircut. Even this trifling amount of autonomy can be built upon.

Up From Boredom, Down From Fear

In the beginning it is always best to concentrate on what you do have, rather than bemoaning what you lack. Do you have complete control, for example, over how you spend the fifty dollars Aunt Elsie gave you for your birthday? Can you sleep in on Saturday morning if you feel like it? Do you really care if your lawn isn't as well combed as your neighbor's? Would your husband mind if you never went to the Wednesday Night Bingo Game again? What *can* you do?

The answer, of course, is that your life is yours to mold as you will. And the more you do it, the better you get. Interesting people don't get pushed around nor do they have to push others. Bored people get pushed around either by other people or their own Crazy Me's. With practice you'll soon find yourself learning to self-regulate your mental and emotional states in such a way that you'll be able to bring yourself up from boredom and down from fear at will. Your Sane Me will become the constant companion your Crazy Me once was.

Interesting people are in control of their thoughts and feelings. Guilt, fear and worry run amok in the bored person. When these crazy voices dominate your Sane Me and you're overwhelmed by negative thoughts and emotions, it feels as if there's no way out. There's nothing more upsetting than this loss of self-control.

One of the most popular and most destructive psychological notions now in vogue is the wisdom of indulging these thoughts and feelings and venting them on whoever happens to be handy, including yourself. This kind of behavior is like a person with a weight problem or a drinking problem going on a bender. It only makes things worse. The idea got started when people began to recognize that they were out of touch with their feelings; the obvious solution seemed to be to encourage people to experience

268

these feelings and express them. Unfortunately, once you've learned what they are, you still have them. Simply venting them doesn't seem to get rid of them.

Interesting people are not only in touch with their feelings, they also know how to keep the less desirable ones from running away with them. They've learned to listen to their crazy voices and talk back to them before they gain control and manipulate them into doing, thinking and feeling things that are not at all in their own best interests.

Interesting people stay on an even keel. Part and parcel of learning how to control yourself is learning to keep yourself on an even keel—not getting swept up into fear by your negative feelings or, perhaps worse, down into boredom because you haven't laid anything on the line. People who are excited by living have learned how to find their optimal level of arousal and stay there. They can remain open to new sources of stimulation, and can keep their lives in a state of constant flux and change, without getting overstimulated. They know how to make trouble for themselves without crossing the line into fear.

What distinguishes a good athlete from a "bad" one is not necessarily the individual's skill, but his ability to know his or her limits and to play within them. Interesting people are psychological athletes. Accepting and looking for enough action to keep you stimulated without taking on too much is the hallmark of the person who is neither bored nor boring.

Interesting people make their own rules. They don't, however, make them simply to be obstinate or to walk all over someone else. They make them in self-defense, knowing that they need their own guidelines to operate by—that what works for someone else probably won't work for them. Because of this self-governing capacity, interesting

269

people are generally quite independent of others. They're not aloof, not frightened, they don't demand more than they are willing to give; they're simply attuned to relationships of interdependence and healthy give-and-take between people. They've learned to shun the dependency and emotional blackmail that comes from allowing anyone else to dominate or dictate their lives.

Interesting people are self-starters. Constantly growing and changing, their flexibility is part of the ongoing process of creating their own individuality—an individuality they express rather than hide. Their personal search and the uniqueness of their discoveries make them interesting, their involvement with life makes them an exciting and powerful force to be with.

Interesting people have a vast emotional, intellectual and behavioral repertoire. In creating themselves or, more accurately, in letting their sane selves be, they develop interests, needs, values, behaviors, attitudes and feelings that, to the "average" person, seem to be incongruously juxtaposed. This is why creative people are often thought to border on insanity. They are willing to put things together in very unusual and peculiar ways . . . ways that are their own, but ways that work. They surprise you with their unpredictability. They are exciting to be around. They truly hear the sound of a different drummer . . . their own drummer . . . your own drummer. They are people of vision. They are people who don't give up. They've been knocked down either despite their individuality or because of it, yet they continue to get up again, and again, and again. . . . They're troublemakers because they won't stay down. They reach out. They're doing what they want to be doing. Their lives are together. They're not missing out.

270

We all would like to be described by others as an "interesting" person. But this is really putting the cart before the horse. For to interest others, we must first be interesting to ourselves. Being interesting is merely the other side of the boredom coin.

Remember: If you're not bored, you're not boring. It's as simple as that. People who get to know themselves, who refuse to let guilt and fear run their lives, and who choose to act on their own behalf, draw other people like magnets. In other words, if you've taken to heart the experimental attitude toward life I've described and—what's more important—put it into practice, you need never worry about whether or not you're interesting to others. In fact, you probably won't even have the time or the inclination to consider the question.

This book is full of splendid advice. But I would be the last person on earth to tell you to accept it at face value. I would ask you to test out some of these techniques for eliminating boredom, however, simply because if you are genuinely among the bored, I'm sure you'll agree that you have nothing left to lose and everything to gain. I would ask you to try earnestly to discover the sources of your discontent and to separate, as best you can, fact from fiction, the sane you from the crazy you.

Boredom is perhaps the most personal malady there is; it thrives on one's ignorance of one's self, on early fears and imaginings. It finds a permanent niche in unexamined lives. It diminishes the wonder of everything around us. But once you've learned to escape from boredom, you'll never look back.

"Be yourself," wrote Max Ehrmann, the Indiana poet. "Especially, do not feign affection. Neither be cynical about love; for in the face of all aridity and disenchantment

271

it is perennial as the grass. Take kindly the counsel of the years, gracefully surrendering the things of youth. Nurture strength of spirit to shield you in sudden misfortune. But do not distress yourself with imaginings. Many fears are born of fatigue and loneliness. Beyond a wholesome discipline, be gentle with yourself. You are a child of the universe, no less than the trees and the stars; *you have a right to be here.*"